AF576503

# OLD TOURAINE

A compelling history of the castles of France and their inhabitants, this comprehensive work details the geography and history of French castles, the influences of feudalism and of women, literary associations with castles, dungeons and torture chambers, and the building of castles. Among the historical figures which feature in the book are Joan of Arc, the Abbey of Fontevrault and the Dukes of Orleans.

**www.keganpaul.com**

# THE KEGAN PAUL TRAVELLERS SERIES

A Journey Through Persia and Turkish Armenia • *Gerald Reitlinger*
A Summer in Touraine • *Frederic Lees*
A Winter in Majorca • *George Sand*
A Woman in the Balkans • *Winifred Gordon*
Adventure in Hawaii and Tahiti • *Edward T. Perkins*
Alexandria: The Ancient and Modern Town • *E. Breccia*
Autobiography of a Chinese Girl • *Hsieh Ping-Ying*
Burma • *R. Talbot Kelly*
Chinese Pictures • *J. F. Bishop*
Egypt and Nubia • *J. A. St. John*
Fifty Years in Maoriland • *James T. Pinfold*
In Hawaii with Jack London • *Jack London*
In Stevenson's Samoa • Marie Fraser
Island Nights' Entertainments • *Robert Louis Stevenson*
Man and Animals in the New Hebrides • *John R. Baker*
Mongolia • *N. Prejevalsky*
My Consulate in Samoa • *William B. Churchward*
News from Tartary • *Peter Fleming*
Oceania • *Frank Fox*
Unbeaten Tracks in Japan • *Isabella Lucy Bird*
Old Touraine • *Theodore Andrea Cook*
The Discovery of Tahiti • *George Robertson*
The French Riviera • *Pierre Devoluy and Pierre Borel*
The Golden Chersonese • Isabella Lucy Bird
The Heart of the Orient • *Michael Myers Shoemaker*
The Riviera • *Hugh Macmillan*
The Romance of Treasure Trove • *Charles R. Beard*
To Lhasa in Disguise • *William Montgomery McGovern*
Treasure of Ophir • C. E. V. Craufurd
A Year Amongst the Persians • *Edward Granville Browne*
Constantinople and Istanbul Old and New • *H. G. Dwight*
Tahiti • *George Calderon*
Cruise of the Snark • *Jack London*
In the South Seas • *Robert Louis Stevenson*
Six Months in Hawaii • *Isabella Bird*
Korea and Her Neighbours • *Isabella Bird*
Strolling Through Istanbul • *H. Sumner-Boyd and J. Freely*
Camp Life and Sport in Dalmatia and the Herzegovina • *Anonymous*
Quest for Sheba • *Norman Stone Pearn and Vernon Barlow*
An English Consul in Siam • *W. A. R. Wood*
Voyages in the Orient • *Gerald De Nerval*
The Loyal Karens of Burma • *Donald Mackenzie Smeaton*
Romance of a Harem • *Clarence Forestier-Walker*
South Sea Idyls • *Charles Warren Stoddard*
Hawaii: The Past, Present and Future of its Island-Kingdom • *Gerald Manly Hopkins*

Drawing from a bust in terra-cotta of a Magistrate in Touraine of the sixteenth century, probably by Michel Columbe, now in the possession of M. Mélizet, La Péraudière, Tours.
(*Reproduced by permission of M. Péricat, Tours.*)

# OLD TOURAINE

THE LIFE AND HISTORY
OF THE
FAMOUS CHATEAUX OF FRANCE

VOLUME I

THEODORE ANDREA COOK

KEGAN PAUL
London • New York • Bahrain

First published in 2004 by
Kegan Paul Limited
UK: P.O. Box 256, London WC1B 3SW, England
Tel: 020 7580 5511 Fax: 020 7436 0899
E-Mail: books@keganpaul.com
Internet: http://www.keganpaul.com
USA: 61 West 62nd Street, New York, NY 10023
Tel: (212) 459 0600 Fax: (212) 459 3678
Internet: http://www.columbia.edu/cu/cup
BAHRAIN: bahrain@keganpaul.com

Distributed by:
Extenza-Turpin
Stratton Business Park
Pegasus Drive
Biggleswade, Bedfordshire SG18 8QB
United Kingdom
Tel: (01462) 672555 Fax: (01462) 480947
Email: books@extenza-turpin.com

Columbia University Press
61 West 62nd Street, New York, NY 10023
Tel: (212) 459 0600 Fax: (212) 459 3678
Internet: http://www.columbia.edu/cu/cup



Printed in the USA by IBT/Biddles



ISBN: 0-7103-0989-9

**British Library Cataloguing in Publication Data**
A catalogue record for this book is available from the British Library.

**Library of Congress Cataloging-in-Publication Data**
Applied for.

# PREFACE

"Pour l'instruction de l'Univers Sédentaire."
XAVIER LE MAISTRE.

THE chapters which follow have been arranged on the only plan by which it seemed logically possible to sketch the great amount of history with which they have to deal: it may be as well to point out the way in which they are meant to be of use.

Each castle in the valley of the Loire has a history of its own, sometimes going as far back as Roman times, sometimes reaching forward to the present day; but in each castle there is also some particular event, some especial visitor, whose importance overshadows every memory connected with the place; it therefore became possible to arrange these "moments" chronologically, and thus gradually to unwind a more or less connected thread of history from the rise of the Angevin Plantagenets where Chinon guards the bridge of the Vienne to the last days of the Valois in the Château of Blois. In some cases the story has been carried on by chapters on the more important personages, such as the earlier Dukes of Orleans or Marguerite de Valois, but anything approaching to thorough treatment of so long a period in one book was impossible. This arrangement of the mass of details which had to be in some way dealt with, seemed to recommend itself both from its utility to the traveller in the valley of the Loire, and from its clearness in the presentment of a certain side of French history to that large portion of the cultivated universe which, like M. le Maistre, is wont to do its travelling at home.

> "Could any spot of earth
> Show to his eye an image of the pangs
> Which it hath witnessed, render back an echo
> Of the sad steps by which it hath been trod." . . .

Characters will perhaps gain in reality for the reader, scenes may be imagined with a greater vividness, when described in their actual setting. "The stone shall cry out of the wall, and the beam out of the timber shall answer it."

The materials used have been first and foremost the rich mine of original authorities published in the *Documents Inédits*, the collection of *Mémoires* by Petitot, and the smaller transcripts by Zeller from the Memoirs and Letters of the time, which are in a more portable form and of distinct value. Among more modern authorities I have referred to the *Histories* of Michelet and of Martin, and the *Analyse Raisonnée* of Châteaubriand; for Chapter II. to K. Norgate's *Angevin Kings*; for episodes at Chinon and at Blois to Yriarte's *Cæsar Borgia* and the Stanhope Essay for 1891; to *Un Gentilhomme des temps passés* and *François I.* by C. Coignet; and to *The End of the Middle Ages* and *Marguerite of Navarre* by Madame James Darmesteter, to whose invaluable suggestions I have been very much indebted throughout the whole work. On questions of architecture, Petit's *Architectural Studies*, the wonderfully complete works of Viollet le Duc, and the *Renaissance of Art in France* by Mrs. Mark Pattison, have been consulted. A list in the Appendix has collected a few other authorities upon various subjects. Much help has doubtless been obtained elsewhere, but it is not wittingly left unacknowledged. All of the guide-books which are published for each château have been freely used, and in recognising my obligations to their various authors I would especially single out the accurate and conscientious productions of Mgr. Chevalier, whose publications from the archives of Chenonceaux are particularly valuable, and lastly, the researches of M. de la Saussaye in the history of the Château of Blois and its neighbourhood.

I am assured that the materials at present collected have never been published in one book before either in France or England ; the need for them in a portable form for travellers in Touraine is certainly a distinct one, and it is hoped that the illustrations will still further increase the interest of Englishmen in a province, once an English possession, whose history has so much in common with their own. I have especially to thank M. Péricat of the Rue de la Scellerie, Tours, for allowing me to reproduce several plates from a book of which he has lately published a few copies, and which forms the finest collection yet extant of the best types of art in Touraine. The earlier chapters of Mr. Henry James's *Little Tour in France*, full of happy suggestion and a keen artistic sense, will show the traveller the right way to use his eyes; Mgr. Chevalier's *Guide Pittoresque du Voyageur en Touraine* will give him further details and still more extend his wanderings ; Mrs. Mark Pattison's *Renaissance in France* will point out for him all that is most valuable in Tours and in Touraine of architecture, painting, and sculpture. These three books will also give all the information required concerning the town of Tours itself, its possibilities of pleasure, its facilities for locomotion, its unequalled surroundings.

In the Appendix I have inserted a few points which would have overcrowded the text, but which seemed necessary to give completeness to the work ; among them is a note on the Library of Tours furnished for me by the kindness of the librarian, M. Duboz. The first division of the Appendix collects some additional points of interest in the town of Tours itself and in Touraine ; the second is a list of the manuscripts and books in the various public libraries of the town ; the third deals with the numerous portraits and pictures (chiefly of the school of the Clouets) to be seen in Touraine and elsewhere in France and England, that bear upon the portion of history treated ; in the last is added a further list of books and manuscripts which may be used where more facts are needed than I have been able to reproduce.

From lack of space much has been omitted that may afterwards appear, should the want for it seem pressing. I have, however, been able to add a Genealogical Table, which includes all the more important families in France who had any connection with Touraine, and a Map which is reduced from the sheets of the French Government Survey, and will show the relative position of the places mentioned, several of which are considerably beyond the boundaries of Touraine, accurately so called. From this map it will be seen that three centres of exploration should be made by the traveller in the valley. The first, Saumur, from which he can drive to Fontevrault and Chinon, then go by rail to Azay-le-Rideau, and by rail or road return to Tours ; the second, Tours, from which three excursions are possible—(1) by road along the Loire to Luynes, Cinq Mars, and Langeais, and thence home by train ; (2) by rail past Montbazon to Loches ; (3) by rail to Amboise, thence to Chenonceaux, and home by rail ; his third centre will be Blois ; from here he can drive to Chambord and return by the Château of Cheverny, and the next day follow the road along the Loire to Chaumont, and drive back through the Forest of Russy, past the Château of Beauregard, and so to Blois. Throughout the province the hotels are good, the wines sound, the roads excellent, and a great deal can be done on horseback or in a light carriage ; the trains are slow but conscientious, and by the various lines will take the traveller who is wise enough to be leisurely, to almost any place he may desire to visit.

In conclusion, I take this opportunity of expressing my deep sense of the courtesy and assistance so freely rendered me on every side during my stay in Touraine, and more especially I would acknowledge the great help given me in many ways by M. James Darmesteter ; to him and to several friends in Oxford I owe most of what is useful in this attempt ; its shortcomings are my own.

T. A. C.

19 Merton Street,
Oxford.

# CONTENTS

## CHAPTER III



## CHAPTER IV



## CHAPTER V

## CHAPTER VI



## CHAPTER VII



## CHAPTER VIII

## CHAPTER IX



## CHAPTER X



## CHAPTER XI

# LIST OF ILLUSTRATIONS

> "Nothing is there to come, and nothing past,
> But an eternal now does always last."

---

δοκεῖ γὰρ εἶναί τι τῷ τεθνεῶτι καὶ κακὸν καὶ ἀγαθόν.

---

BENEATH the lime trees on the terrace walk
I sat, and watched the silver of the moon
Slip softly from the river to the sands
That fringe with pale gold bars the silent Loire.
The busy chirping of the insect wings,
That all day long had rustled in the sun,
Was still ; the tiny lizards on the wall,
That all day long had flitted to and fro
The burning stones, had vanished ; sweetly fell
A silvern silence on the shadowed fields
Where scarce a blade of grass bent to the breeze,
The gentle breeze of evenings in Touraine
Which comes but to caress the weary brow
And breathe contentment ; from the darker line,
Where the soft grey of heaven kissed the earth,
The moon rose higher to the cloudless blue
And touched with light the tall Cathedral Towers,
That like twin sisters rose above the trees
Crowned with the evening star.

There came a sound
More felt than heard, as of the rustling wings
Of countless souls that moved in upper air
Or glided with the moonbeams through the night ;
Souls of the dead who visited the homes
Where once they dwelt ; and some sought all in vain,
And some who found seemed sorrowful to find,
Or, with a horror of remembered sin
Pursuing them, shuddered and passed alone ;
And some few, near the old Cathedral Towers,
Rested awhile in peace, as though to kiss
A treasured memory within the stones.
Softly the echoes from the far-off bell
Whispered along the river, and the souls
All gathered, so methought, within the fane,
And joined their silent prayers with those below
Who sang thanksgivings ; all the vault of night
Seemed full of harmonies that rose and fell
Till they were caught up to the heaven above
And borne amid the company of souls
From lesser lights to higher, where the stars
Bent down to listen.
So the future seemed
To mingle with the past. For a short space
I saw revealed the double threads that bind
This little speck of time we call "To-day"
To the great cycle of unending life
That has been and that shall be evermore.

TRIANON, ST SYMPHORIEN,
TOURS.

# CHAPTER I

## INTRODUCTORY

### EARLY HISTORY OF TOURAINE

"With kings and counsellors of the earth, which built desolate places for themselves; or with princes that had gold, who filled their houses with silver."

THE old province of Touraine very nearly corresponds

to the modern department of the Indre et Loire, though in some directions it is rather more extended. It is crossed from east to west by the rapid and sandy stream of the Loire, which flows through it for a distance of some ninety kilometres from a point not far above Amboise to the valley of Fontevrault. The three chief tributaries of the Loire, at this part of its course, join the river from its southern side; and with very few exceptions it is with this left-hand bank of the stream that we shall chiefly have to do, our limits being Chambord to the east, in the department of the Loir et Cher, and to the west Saumur, in the old province of Anjou, the modern department of the Maine et Loire.

In the forests to the north and east of Blois are the Châteaux of Chambord, of Cheverny, and Beauregard; while farther to the south and west is Chaumont looking down upon the Loire, which there flows beneath the ramparts of Amboise westward to the cathedral towers of Tours. Upon the right bank, farther down, are Luynes, Cinq Mars, and Langeais; and the Cher, which near here flows from the south-east into the Loire, has passed the galleries of Chenonceaux, some sixty kilometres from its mouth. The southern waters of the Indre are guarded by the rugged keep of Loches, and by Montbazon farther westward, and finally wind in and out among the trees that shade Azay-le-Rideau, before losing themselves in the swifter current of the main stream. At Candes the river is still further swollen by the Vienne, which after passing the ruined towers of Chinon has flowed by the Forest of Fontevrault to add its story to the many voices of the Loire.

Perhaps no stream in so short a portion of its course has so much history to tell. Until the end of the sixteenth century this part of France was covered with a multitude of châteaux, for beside the old feudal towers, whose strength had saved them from destruction in the happier times of peace, the nobles of later days had raised more elegant abodes, in which they strove to preserve only what had been picturesque in the earlier fortified dwellings. By the wars of religion and the disturbances of the Fronde a great number of the châteaux had been ruined or defaced : by the line of policy which was begun by Louis XI. and carried on by Henry IV. to receive its full development at the hands of Richelieu and Louis XIV., the old feudal spirit had been finally crushed ; even architecture took an entirely different form.

The Court, which for so many centuries had moved to and fro among the pleasant castles of Touraine, migrated towards Paris, and filled the wide walks and never-ending gardens of Versailles and Fontainebleau : the last of the old feudal barons was Agrippa d'Aubigné, the friend and comrade in arms of Henry of Navarre, who kept his fortresses till he left France, and then sold them to the Rohans. By the Revolution the old châteaux were within an ace of being destroyed for ever ; the "crown of Cybele" in Touraine lost nearly half its beauty, for with changing times the life of other centuries perished, and "like an unsubstantial pageant faded," though legends of it and memories of it still cling to the ruined walls like the ivy which a kindly soil has lent to hide their falling gateways. It is true that here and again a new life mingles with the old, but many of the ancient homes stand empty and deserted, or, saddest fate of all, await richer purchasers to save them from destruction.

Chenonceaux is in the grip of a great Paris company ; in Amboise, where Abd-el-Kader chafed in prison, where Marie Stuart sighed over the slaughtered Huguenots, no courtly laughter comes again to grace the mutilated halls, for the Orleans princes abode there but a little while, and have left it dead again. Loches seems happier as the seat of a Sous-Préfet, who dwells by the tomb of Agnes Sorel ; Plessis-lez-Tours is worst changed of all. The churches of the Middle Ages live on still and have a meaning for us even in their ruins, for the faith that built them is among us still ; but the feudal castles belong to a life and a time so different from our own that to understand them at all we must go back to the history of which they formed a part ; we must try, as well and shortly as may be, to people these walls that are still echoing with a larger and a fuller life than ours, to realise the men who built them and lived in them, to imagine for ourselves that dead and gone feudalism in the midst of which the youth of the French nation grew hard and strong.

Nor is it difficult to discover a reason for the interest and fascination which the modern world finds, and will always find, in that old life : we are perpetually receiving pleasant shocks from its astounding originality, from the unexpected nature of its modes of thought and action. An age unfettered by the later restrictions of what is called society, by a morality from which it results that the actions of any given man in any given position can often be accurately foretold, a generation which was innocent of Kant, and ignorant of Herbert Spencer, could well preserve a spontaneity and freshness of impulse, an individuality of method and resource which is as strange as it is fascinating to men of a later and more conventional society ; for the passions of its barbarism mingle in curious ways with lighter fantasies of the imagination, with a deeper and more heartfelt poetic feeling. But in this very freedom of the feudal age lay the germs of its decay. The system that liberated the warriors of the time from all the higher bonds imposed by the idea of Nationality had placed in society a principle of anarchy that was incompatible with the existence of a great country, that favoured private civil wars, that made a national resistance impossible, and was the source of the terrible disasters of the Hundred Years' War. William the Conqueror, at the conquest of England, had discovered long before the rest of France the defects of the old system, and had broken the mould of Feudalism ;[1] it was one of the many signs of his greatness that he had done so.

There is yet another fact which, while it adds

[1] C. Coignet, *François I.*

one more reason for our interest in these early days, is itself the mainspring of much of their hot-blooded impulse and versatile emotion: in no other country have women exercised so great an influence upon politics and the whole life of the people as in France. It has been truly said that they have avenged the passing of the Salic law; but they have done more: throughout French history, even down to modern times, the motto which guides the historian's researches is "Cherchez la Femme." From the heroine of Charles VII. down to the grand-daughter of that Agrippa d'Aubigné already mentioned, their ambition and their influence for good or evil have been exhibited by women who understood better than those of any other nation how to wield the weapons peculiar to their sex. It is the same in later as in earlier times. "The vice of the sixteenth century," says Michelet, "is the unrestrained outburst of its passion, its blind desire for physical enjoyment, which outraged what it loved." The reaction was a matter of course. The skilful wit of woman and her "sweet reasonableness" laid hold upon this strong brutality and governed it. The sixteenth century was the reign of woman; from the days when the Pisan girls surrounded Charles's army and melted their hard hearts to tears, to the *escadron volant* of the Valois Court, it is by women that the century is troubled, corrupted, civilised. Even in Merovingian times the loves and hates of Fredegonde and of Brunhilda [1] gave a theme to poets of Touraine, and at the very beginning of the period with which these chapters chiefly deal we have three such opposing influences as the shameless Isabel of Bavaria, the Maid of Orleans, and Agnes Sorel. Immediately after Louis XI.'s death the masculine firmness and ability of his daughter Anne de Beaujeu is replaced by the quiet womanly tenacity of the twice-crowned little Breton Queen. The baneful influence Louise de Savoie exercised over her son Francis was but half counteracted by the gentleness and mysticism of his sister Marguerite: Francis was the plaything of his mistresses. The next reign is indeed the reign of a woman. Diane de Poitiers, Duchess of Valentinois, was ruler of the destinies of France, and powerful enough even to crush the venomous Italian Queen into subjection for a time; but the day of Catherine of Medicis was not long in coming, and for three more reigns her hand was at the throat of France, her influence poisoning its Court. Many more notable women there are—Marie Stuart and La Reine Margot, Gabrielle d'Estrées, and yet another Medicis but little better than the first and far less wise, until we come to Louise de la Vallière, and see among the mistresses of Louis XIV. the widow of Scarron standing apart, "the most influential woman of French history," Madame de Maintenon, who was to be the lawful wife of the King.

[1] See Thierry's *Récits Mérovingiens*.

All of these has Touraine welcomed at some time or another, to one of its many palaces, beneath the soft sunshine of the Loire valley, where energy and sustained action seem a thing contrary to nature, in the country of Rabelais, the home of Royal favourites, the afternoon-land of idleness and laughter. Here the grass is as green in August as in May among the orchards and the groves. Look across the river at the other bank and it will seem hanging in the air, so faithfully is cloud and sky reflected in the stream. The sands that line the river's bed are fringed with willows bending down as if to sip its waters ; poplars, aspens, and acacias shade the stream, where countless little islets break the silver current. As Victor Hugo sang of Bièvre—

> " Une rivière au fond, des bois sur les deux pentes,
> Là des orneaux brodés de cent vignes grimpantes
> Des prés où le faucheur brunit son bras nerveux,
> Là des saules pensifs qui pleurent sur la rive
> Et comme une baigneuse indolente et naïve
> Laissent tremper dans l'eau le bout de leurs cheveux."

A soft and sensual country is it, where the idea came naturally to D'Arbrissel to make a woman queen of his monastery.[1]

Nor are these memories of men and women who have lived the only ones with which Touraine is filled ; scarcely less real, and with an added charm

[1] Michelet, vol. ii.

from the genius of their creators, are the characters from Balzac, from Rabelais, from Georges Sand that moved and had their being in the valley—and English readers will before all recognise the scenes in which young Quentin Durward played his part, the postern gate through which he rode out of Plessis with the Ladies of Croye, so soon to be pursued by Dunois and Orleans. Chenonceaux reminds us of "Les Huguenots" as much as of Diana. The halls of Chambord are still crowded with the courtiers watching Marion Delorme, and in the streets of Blois there stands the lamp-post beneath which her lover fought his duel and was taken by the King's officers. There is scarce an abbey in Touraine but finds its own story among the Contes Drolatiques, not a landscape but has its more delicate associations with a Félix or a Lucien, even a Duchesse de Langeais. The very house where the terrible old maid who tortured the Curé de Tours resided, rises hard by the cathedral walls with the great buttress encroaching upon its quiet garden close. Dumas' musketeers are laughing in the Salle des Gardes at Blois, and the rattle of their swords as they fence upon the staircases is ringing even in the King's chambers beyond; and Athos' house might still be seen, to which Raoul rode out from Blois after a certain stolen interview with a young lady distrusted by his father. Jean Jacques Rousseau has wandered in the groves of Chenonceaux;

Madame de Staël has watched the widening Loire at Chaumont. The brilliant pamphlets of Paul Louis Courier come into our mind in the little town of Luynes; at Loches we recall De Vigny's vivid romance and the fall of the unhappy Cinq Mars.

Near Blois,

> "Cette maison
> Qu'on voit, bâtie en pierre, et d'ardoise couverte,
> Blanche et carrée, au bas de la colline verte,"

is the house where Victor Hugo spent his childhood. In endless ways the genius of the place has been embodied and personified. Rabelais is full of touches of the true spirit of Touraine, the life of plenty, and the love of wine, and midday siestas in the autumn sun of good fat priests, their paunches "with fat capon lined," in abbeys that were his models for the great vision of Thelema.

Such is the Touraine to the early history of which we must now turn, and first to its focal point the town of Tours. If there is one thing for which Tours is famous it is for its soldier-saint and the victory of Charles Martel. In 718 the Arabs, who held nearly the whole of Spain, poured over the Pyrenees into the Narbonese district; they were driven back by Odo from Toulouse and from Provence, but they sacked Autun in the South Vosges, and in 732 Abd-el-Rahman, the commander of the Khalif's army in Spain, took Bordeaux, ravaged Aquitaine, and advanced to the plunder of the rich see of St. Martin at Tours. At this time the town was united with the rest of Gaul, and the vigorous Charles Martel was Mayor of the Palace; he led out his small forces against the advancing squadrons of the Infidels, and between Tours and Poitiers (the exact spot is not known) "the young civilisations of Europe and Asia stood face to face," the scimitar of the Eastern horseman tried conclusions with the broadsword of the West. One of the decisive battles in the world's history was won by Charles Martel; the incredible number of 30,000 Arabs are reported to have fallen with their leader, and the Saracens were finally driven out of the midst of France.

But there was a Tours before Charles Martel, although its history does not go back (like that of Langeais and Amboise[1]) before the Roman conquest. Its early name Cæsarodunum first occurs in the Itinerary of Antonine, and by the third century it is already a free State, the Civitas Turonum; the inscriptions proving this were discovered in 1711 on the old foundations of the city wall, which are still to be seen in the cellars of the archbishop's palace.

Of this Roman time we can distinguish two periods: the first, some three centuries of ease and prosperity;[2] the second, a time of military

[1] Langeais (Alingavia), Amboise (Ambacia), Chinon (Caino), and Candes (Candate) are of Gallic origin. See E. Mabille, *Bibl. de l'école des Chartes*, 3me Serie, Art. "Touraine."

[2] For details of the costume about this period see the carvings on the tomb of the Consul Torinus at Rheims, showing the Gallo-Roman

occupation, of fighting which was to last for many years, when new walls were hurriedly reared out of the débris of the older and more peaceful town which extended over the ground covered by the château, the cloisters of St. Gatien, and the Archevêché. The ruined walls of the fifteenth century may still be seen, in fragments, with the capitals and carvings hastily built into them, as Pericles built the long walls from Athens to the Piræus: they lasted until 1202, with the addition of some strengthening towers which looked out over the vines and gardens that covered what is now the Rue Royale.

This Cæsarodunum was the cradle of Gaulish Christianity;[1] St. Gatien had been one of seven missionaries sent out from Rome to evangelise the Gallic provinces; St. Lidorius, the second bishop, began the Cathedral Church in memory of his predecessor. This cathedral, the oldest foundation in Touraine, was dedicated to St. Maurice until the thirteenth century. The first building was burnt in 561 and rebuilt by Gregory. After the fire of 1166 the present structure was begun in 1170; by 1260 the greater part was finished and definitely dedicated to St. Gatien; in 1426 the twin towers were begun,

knight going hunting with spear and hound, clad in short tunic and buskin, with the shoulder-clasped cloak, which recalls the memory of the great centurion's charity.

[1] It also formed the centre of a system by which the great Roman roads connected and bound together Poitiers, Chartres, Bruges, Orleans, Le Mans, and Angers—in many cases the modern roads follow these lines; there are always traces of the old ones.

and soon afterwards the sculptures of the grand façade were finished, but the larger tower was not completed until 1500 and its sister some fifty years later.

The Romans completed the foundation of French civilisation, and then passed away, but the Roman Church remained. Before the end of the fourth century St. Martin, third and most famous of the bishops of Tours, had left the service of the Emperor Julian to engage under the Christian Cross. From every side, and in great numbers, the pagans poured in to be converted to the faith, and the good bishop was constrained to retreat for rest to his little cell at St. Symphorien, backed by the limestone rock and peering down across the greensward to the river, where later on was to rise the noble Abbey of Marmoutier, whose greatest abbot was the famous Alcuin of York. The immense popularity of St. Martin, both in England and France, is evident from the vast number of legends connected with his name upon the Continent, and from the fact that even after the purging of the Calendar his name remained upon the list of saints recognised by the English Church. The first church dedicated to St. Martin was built by his successor; the next, which was burnt in 994, was rebuilt by Hervé in 1014, and only two towers of it remain, the Tour de l'Horloge and the Tour de Charlemagne, in the Romano-Byzantine style, with traces of restoration in twelfth-century

Gothic. The tomb of St. Martin was the ancient sanctuary, the Delphic oracle of France, the centre of the Merovingian world,[1] where its kings came to question destiny at the shrine round which the Counts of Blois and of Anjou broke so many lances. Mans, Angers, and all Brittany were dependent on the see of Tours, whose canons were the Capets and the Dukes of Burgundy and Brittany, the Count of Flanders and the Patriarch of Jerusalem, the Archbishops of Mayence, of Cologne, and Compostello. At Tours there was a mint for money as good as that at Paris, and in very early times silk and precious tissues were made here of finer fabric than in all the rest of France, until Nantes and Lyons joined the capital in competition with the older centre.

But soon after St. Martin's days, by 419, the Visigoths were in Poitou and Berry, and in a few years the "Tractus Armoricanus" revolted from the yoke of Rome; then the Tourangeaux joining the men of Anjou and Maine entered the great confederacy of rebellion and chased from Touraine the Romans, who by 446 had lost all hold upon the province. Long years of struggle follow between Visigoths and Franks, until in 507 Clovis finally conquered Alaric, and Touraine becomes a province of the Franks, in whose hands it remained with several unimportant changes of ownership for the

[1] Michelet, vol. ii. In Carlovingian times this "centre" of faith and activity was transferred to Anjou.

next two centuries. In the time of Charles Martel the Abbey of St. Martin was in its greatest splendour; there is still a relic left, in the modern library of Tours,[1] of its ancient magnificence and culture, in the Gospel written in gold letters upon vellum, upon which the French kings took their oaths. Half a century later Alcuin, pupil of the Venerable Bede, had been sent for by Charlemagne from Rome to be made Bishop of Tours, and here in his famous school he taught the King's sons, Charles, Pepin, and Louis.[2] In 800, Luitgard, the wife of Charlemagne, the "guardian of her people," was buried in the church of St. Martin.

During the next century Tours was, to her sorrow, again the bulwark of that part of France against invading barbarism, but no Charles Martel was at hand to help, and these new invaders proved more troublesome than the Saracens. The terrible pirates from the North had rowed up the Loire and burned St. Martin's Abbey, and the sacred body of the saint had to be moved out of danger and brought back, tradition says, by one Ingelger in 805. The second "reversion" of the same kind occasioned the legend of the saint's body, borne up by his worshippers,

[1] See note on this library in the Appendix.

[2] See Alcuin's Letters, *Dom Bouquet*, v. 605. He writes to Charlemagne to be allowed to send to England for some books, the "flowers of British learning; so that they may be found not only in the garden close of York, but that Touraine also may have its share in the fruits of Paradise."

having put to flight the armies of the aliens, probably in the actual siege of 903.

At the rebuilding of the city King Charles (the Simple) granted the men of Tours a charter for a fortified borough, subject only, like that of St. Denis at Paris, to its own abbot the Duke of the French. By the side of the old town of St. Gatien, the Cæsarodunum of the Romans, arose the town of St. Martin with its especial wall and moat, the Martinopolis within which Henry II. built his Châteauneuf, and which was only united to its neighbour in 1350 to make a better resistance to the English. Within these walls was the Abbey of St. Martin, where Fulk the Good, Count of Anjou, might so often be seen sitting in his stall next to the Dean. Of the Angevin château, built upon the ruins of the old Roman palace, only the Tour de Guise remains, and a stone preserved in the gardens of the Prefecture carved with what looks like the well-known Pompeiian group of two doves drinking from a cup.[1] A still older structure than this was the Tour du roi Hugon, haunted by the legends of this mythical personage, which was destroyed in the eighteenth century. By an ancestor of Henry II., the Count Eudes II. of Anjou, was built the bridge over the Loire in 1031, of which some remnants are still left upon the right bank: the present bridge was begun in 1765.

[1] This stone has been described with more zeal than accuracy as "the funereal monument of Turnus."

To these Counts of Anjou we must now turn. The sketch of later history in Tours (so far as it is not alluded to in subsequent chapters) will be found in the last chapter on the town, which brings its story shortly down to modern days. The Counts of Anjou are the ancestors of the Plantagenets whom we shall meet at our first castle of Chinon, and it is with their extraordinary rise to power and importance that we have now to deal.

## CHAPTER II

### THE COUNTS OF ANJOU

"Pugnent ipsique nepotesque."—VIRGIL.

FROM the writings of John, a monk of Marmoutier, and Thomas Pactius, Prior of Loches, we hear of one Tortulf, a Breton, who especially distinguished himself by his bold defence of the valleys of Touraine against the pirates; his son Ingelger, already mentioned in connection with the return of St. Martin's body to the church of Tours, married the niece of the Archbishop and took Amboise as his dowry. But later researches [1] cast some doubt on these facts. The first name which may be considered as historically accurate is the reputed son of Ingelger, Fulk the Red, Count of Anjou, who, whatever his ancestors may have been, was the first of a remarkable line of princes, stamped all with a strong family likeness, with the same characteristics of energy and thoroughness, and endowed with very brilliant and varied natural powers crossed by a

[1] Mabille, *loc. cit.* Salmon, *Supplément au recueil des Chroniques de Touraine.*

strange vein of spasmodic and unreasonable piety or superstition.

The little kingdom of Anjou, given to its first counts by Odo of Paris in reward for their services against the dreaded pirates, was wedged in between the Loire, the Sarthe, and the Mayenne, and in the hands of less energetic owners would have been inevitably swallowed up in the possessions of the powerful Counts of Blois, had not these latter shown as much of irresolution and weakness as their life-long opponents possessed of keen and unwearying activity. Alone of all his race the second Count, Fulk the Good, waged no wars and took but little part in politics: of him is related the story that when on his way to Tours from his own province he met a leper desiring to be carried to the shrine of St. Martin; the good Fulk lifted up the loathsome burden which every other passer-by had refused, and bore him on his shoulders to the shrine, where the leper vanished; and it was revealed to Fulk, as he was sitting in the choir of the church he loved so well, that the leper was the Christ Himself. His son, Geoffrey Greygown, was of a more martial character, and helped Hugh Capet to his throne before he was laid to rest with his father in the Church of St. Martin.

It is about this time that we meet with legends of an Angevin Count having married a lady of surpassing beauty and somewhat doubtful antecedents, not unconnected with the lower world. The myth is probably an attempt to explain the strange character of the next Count, the typical Angevin, Fulk Nerra, the Black Falcon, who must have been a standing enigma to his contemporaries. In this strange being men saw wonderingly " mad bursts of passion which would have been the ruin of an ordinary man, but which seem scarcely to have made a break in his cool, calculating, far-seeing policy, a rapid and unerring perception of his own ends, a relentless obstinacy in pursuing them." Every town in Touraine has its legend of the Black Count, the great builder beneath whose hands the lower reaches of the Loire gradually bristled with fortresses, that were each one a solid step towards the one dream of his life, the greatness of Anjou. His prowess as a fighter was shown early in the victory of Conquereux, where, in spite of Breton pitfalls, he led his cavalry again and again upon the foe, " as the storm wind sweeps down upon the thick cornrigs." By that victory he secured the lower waters of the Loire. Farther up he held Amboise through his mother's right, and Loches by his wife, and from both places he dashed out upon Touraine against the power of Odo, Count of Blois, in the beginnings of a strife which was but the foreshadowing of the quarrel between Stephen of Blois and Henry of Anjou for the English crown.

In pursuance of a steady policy Fulk built his

fortresses in a long crescent from Angers to Amboise, cutting out Touraine from the domains of Blois; Loudun and Mirebeau menaced Saumur, the border fortress which held the valley of Vienne; Montresor was kept by Roger the Devil, between the Indre and the Cher, on whose banks was the keep of Montrichard; Langeais and Montbazon threatened Tours. From his high tower of Loches, beneath which his son, the future Hammer of Anjou, was being brought up in a blacksmith's forge, the Black Count looked out across the lands of Beaulieu, lit up by the rising sun, and, in a sudden fit of repentance for much bloodshedding, built there, in 1012, an abbey, which was consecrated on his return from one of several visits to the Holy Land undertaken from the same strange spasmodic promptings of irregular religion. Four years later, after several victories over Odo of Blois, he turned his restless arms from Touraine northward to the lands of Maine: it was a momentous change of policy, the first link in the chain that was to stretch across the borders into Normandy and beyond seas to England, until it ended in the marriage of the Empress Matilda to Geoffrey Plantagenet. But for the moment farther advance northward was stopped by a resolute attack from Blois, which the Black Falcon checked with his usual vigour. Swooping upon Saumur, whose master was away near Tours, Fulk seized the valley of the Vienne, retook Montbazon and Langeais, and by finally capturing Chinon, reduced all Touraine, except its capital. Characteristically he left the last task unfinished, went suddenly (for the fourth time) to Jerusalem, and died on his way home near Metz. Until 1793 his tomb was in the Abbey of Beaulieu, and can still, with some amount of certainty, be pointed out.[1]

Geoffrey Martel seemed to have inherited his father's warlike capabilities. He signalised his arrival to power by crushing Aquitaine, and absorbing the territory of Maine after the taking of Le Mans: the possessions of Anjou now touched the Norman boundary. Then, taking up Fulk's unfinished work in Touraine, Geoffrey seized St. Julien and attacked the town of Tours, which, after some severe fighting, he finally captured. But Touraine was not yet to be Angevin, and the conquest of Le Mans now began to bear fruit. In 1048 Duke William of Normandy came to the help of his suzerain the French King and attacked Maine; but a rapid change of policy followed William's too evident and increasing power. It is characteristic of the times that some ten years after we find King Henry at Geoffrey's palace in Angers arranging a combined harrying of the Duchy of Normandy. This failed, as it only deserved to do, and within two years both conspirators were dead.

The County of Anjou now enters upon the

[1] See Salies, *Foulques Nerra*, pp. 456 *seq.* (ref. quoted by Norgate).

saddest portion of its history, the times of the Count Fulk Rechin, who for twenty-eight years kept the rightful heir, Geoffrey, imprisoned in the dungeons of Chinon, until the wretched captive lost all longing for liberty or crown. Nor were other signs of this shameful period any more encouraging. The only bright spot in the dark reigns of Fulk Rechin and of Philip I. is the life of Count Elias of Maine, who for a time saved Le Mans from Norman rule. But with the accession of Louis VI., and after Henry of England, by the victory of Tinchebray, had made himself master of Normandy, better days dawned for Anjou with the marriage of the new Count Fulk to Aremburg the heiress of Maine. The next years are years of fighting with Normandy and England, which resulted in impressing the English King Henry more and more with the strength and capacity of his young Angevin rival. At last, in 1119, Matilda of Anjou was married to William the Aetheling, heir to the English Crown, to whom Fulk shortly after left his kingdom before going to Jerusalem.

But the end was not yet. The youth who would have inherited an undisputed power over England, Normandy, and the possessions of Anjou was drowned in the *White Ship* in November 1120. After the first passion of his grief was over, Henry at once took new measures for the security of the succession to the English crown. His daughter

Matilda, widow of the Emperor Henry V., was acknowledged heiress by the assembled English barons, and sent over to be married amidst great rejoicings to Geoffrey Plantagenet, the handsome son of Fulk, Count of Anjou. All hope for the new Empire of the Angevins now rested on the issue of this marriage, and Fulk, feeling, perhaps, that his day was over and his work in Europe done, was given the cross by Archbishop Hildebert in the Cathedral of Tours, and said good-bye to his daughter, the widow of William the Aetheling, who had retired to the Abbey of Fontevrault. The rest of his family met him for the last time in the same quiet cloisters, and he went away to fight the Turks and Saracens as King of Jerusalem.

Geoffrey Plantagenet, who took his name from the golden broom that brightens the wide fields of Maine and Anjou, was of "a fair and ruddy countenance, lit up by the lightning glance of a pair of brilliant eyes;" his broad shoulders and strong frame were graceful as they were strong and active. Nor were his intellectual attainments less striking, in a time of almost universal ignorance among the fighting barons. Within a few years a son and heir was born to Matilda at Le Mans, the future Henry II., who was to overshadow even his father's strong individuality. Two years later died Henry I. The old quarrel between Anjou and Blois arose again, and was to be far keener, for the stake was a much greater one. Stephen, Count of Boulogne, the first layman in England after the King, was the third son of Stephen, Count of Blois, by his wife, Adela, daughter of the Conqueror. At the King's death he had the immense advantage of being on the spot almost immediately after, though such a tempest arose at his crossing from Boulogne as almost rid the young heir in Anjou of his most dangerous rival.

But at first the outlook seemed black indeed for the child of Geoffrey and Matilda. England they had lost, and Normandy was gone too ; yet the Angevin persistence won at last, helped by the old unsteady nature traditional in the house of Blois. In 1139 Matilda sailed for England with her son, to be received by Robert of Gloucester. Seven years of struggle followed, during which the English Chronicle gives a fearful picture of the sufferings of the land, until, in 1146, Stephen secured his hold upon the English crown. Meanwhile across the Channel Geoffrey of Anjou had taken Normandy, and had been recognised its duke by King Louis VI. The young Henry was then called back to be given the duchy by his father, who died in 1151. As Duke of Normandy and Count of Anjou Henry married Eleanor of Aquitaine and Gascony (who had just been divorced from the French King), and soon prepared to make good his claims to England against the house of Blois.

After crushing at Montsoreau on the Loire a revolt in favour of Eustace, Stephen's son, which had been joined by Henry's own brother Geoffrey, the lord of Chinon, Loudun, and Mirebeau, he found his way made clearer by the death of Eustace in 1153, followed soon after by that of Stephen, and in December 1154, on the Sunday before Christmas, he was crowned as King Henry II. of England in Westminster Abbey, without a single competitor, and with the goodwill of high and low.

Henry Plantagenet had "the square stout form, fiery face, close-cropped hair, prominent eyes, bull neck, coarse and strong hands, bowed legs, that marked out the keen, stirring, coarse-fibred man of business," the man of superhuman activity, above all, whose Court was to be a very pandemonium of energy. His character was a mystery to those who had not known Fulk Nerra and the strange fascination which the clear-headed Black Count combined with unaccountable variations of his temperament; and the puzzled courtiers found yet another character to marvel at in the winning personality and the courageous spirit of Thomas Becket, the unclerical Chancellor. While these two worked together they were the best of friends; and when their interests clashed their hatred was the keener. In 1158, soon after Henry had taken Chinon and all the Angevin possessions from his brother's hands into his own power, a gorgeous embassy arrived with Thomas

Becket at its head, to ask the hand of Margaret, daughter of the King of France, for Henry's eldest son. Four years later Becket was Archbishop of Canterbury, and in 1163 he attended, in great state, a council held by the Pope at Tours.

The quarrel with King Henry had begun. After a vain attempt to settle it by the famous Constitutions of Clarendon, Thomas Becket, much to the delight of the French King, was soon flying for safety to a Cistercian abbey in Burgundy. Meanwhile King Henry's power grew and strengthened on both sides of the Channel. In France, Brittany had been subdued by 1169, and the southern princes who had rebelled after the conference at Chinon were thoroughly crushed into subjection. In the next year Thomas Becket, who had been reconciled to his royal master in the "Traitor's Meadow" on the borders of Vendôme and Chartres, met him again at Tours on his way towards Amboise; it was at Amboise that in Becket's presence Henry wrote to his son to enforce the restoration of the archiepiscopal estates. They met once more at Chaumont, and the primate then returned. On the 29th of December in the same year all Europe was horrified by the news of the Archbishop's murder before the shrine of St. Benedict in the Cathedral of Canterbury. The King's trouble at this cowardly assassination was sincere enough, and was soon increased by signs of the approaching disturbances in his own family, which were to harass his life to the end; but for the moment they ceased; between Tours and Amboise Henry met the rebel princes, and agreed upon a general amnesty.

The years between 1175 and 1182 were those of the greatest prosperity of the Angevin Empire; in the story of Chinon we shall trace its gradual fall. These years of peace left their traces throughout Anjou and Touraine not in donjons or in fortresses, but in palaces, hospitals, bridges, and embankments. A round tower, which stands in the barrack-yard at Tours, is the sole surviving fragment of one of Henry's castles built about this time. The great dyke along the Loire from Ponts de Cé, just above the meeting of the Mayenne and the Loire, for thirty miles eastwards of Bourgueil, was the work of Henry. And the bridge which tradition says was built across the Vienne by the devil for Fulk Nerra when he made his marvellous raid upon Saumur, was in reality the Pont de l'Annonain,[1] a long viaduct built above the level of the floods across river and meadow towards Poitou, to make a safe road from Chinon, Henry's favourite home.[2]

[1] By some authorities called the "Pont aux Nonnains." See chap. on Fontevrault.

[2] For the whole period of this chapter see the *History* of K. Norgate.

## CHAPTER III

### CHINON

"Je sçay," répondit Pantagruel, "où est Chinon et la cave peinte aussy, j'y ay bu maints verres de vin frais et ne fais doute aucun que Chinon ne soit ville antique, son blason l'atteste auquel est dit deux ou trois fois

Chinon
Petite ville grand renom
Assise sus pierre ancienne
Au haut le bois au pied la Vienne.

"Mais comment seroit elle ville première du monde ? où le trouvez vous par écrit ? quelle conjecture en avez ?"

PANTAGRUEL suggested that the derivation of Chinon, or Caynon, as he sometimes called it, was from Cain its first founder ;[1] but the stern accuracy of later philologists will have it that "Chinon" is derived from "*blanc*" or brilliant, from the sparkling waters of the Vienne.

[1] See Mabille, *loc. cit.* The old name of Chinon was Caino, of Gallic origin. Professor Rhys tells me that in North Wales there is a place called by the Celtic name of *Cain*, which comes from the same

In the course of our journey from Tours, where we had left the Loire behind us only to cross the waters of the Cher, the slowness of the train gave us more than sufficient time to thoroughly grasp the features of the country, to fully imbibe what Balzac calls "le sentiment du beau qui respire dans le paysage de Tours," where "in spring love flies at large beneath the open sky, . . . in autumn the air is full of memories of those who are no more." Soon we passed Ballan, where in the Château de la Carte lived Jacques de Beaune Semblançay, the unfortunate victim of the anger of Louise de Savoie; we shall hear more of this shameful transaction later on. Then came Miré with its traditions of Charles Martel and the defeated Saracens, then the third river on our route, the Indre, whose winding channels reflect the sculptured galleries of Azay-le-Rideau. We were passing through the country in which Félix found his "Lys dans la Vallée," passing "the long-drawn ribbon of the stream that sparkles in the sun between its two green banks, the lines of poplars draping with the flutter of their lace this valley of the Loire, the chestnut trees that stand between the vineyards on the sloping hills." With due slowness and precision our train at last stopped at Chinon on the banks of the Vienne. The first step into the little square beyond the station gates

root as the German schön. But no derivations are so difficult as those of Proper Names.

showed us we had had the happiness to arrive on one of the great market-days at the end of September; we found afterwards it was the most important market of the year.

The roads were closed in with tall trees whose sides were cut with somewhat frigid exactitude in lines parallel to the direction of the pavement; they were full of country girls brown-cheeked and black-eyed, arrayed in the picturesque lace caps of their province; booths of every kind were full of busy traffic; skeleton men and fat women in their fullest glory were disputing for attention with tiny travelling theatres and vendors of malodorous refreshment. No one seemed in any particular hurry to do anything; so, imitating the frame of mind of the inhabitants, we aimlessly strolled up the long straight road towards the bridge that spans the reddish waters of the river. Here the press grew thicker, and round the statue of Rabelais was a gay crowd of buyers and sellers, of laughing girls and chattering children, carts and donkeys laden with country produce, geese and chickens dead and alive, the very scene of busy happiness and careless human nature that Rabelais himself enjoyed and described too, when he tells how Couillatris goes to Chinon, "ville noble ville antique voyre première du monde," to buy oxen, cows and sheep, pigs, capon, geese, and a whole catalogue of sound comestibles. The statue is a far finer production than the one at Tours, whose face with its eternal smile pleases perhaps at first sight, but soon degenerates into little more than simpering monotony. On the face of the Rabelais of Chinon there is all the possibility of laughter, as there is the possibility of satire ; and in this lies the superiority of the statue : upon the mouth of the true Rabelais—the mouth of a cultivated Silenus—there was anything rather than an eternal smile, though none of his time knew better how to lead a laugh and keep it going ; upon that face there must have been the traces of the great human feeling, all the love of human liberty which was Rabelais' great characteristic, and which only assumed the cap and bells of Folly to secure a hearing or to be sure of safety. He was born at Chinon in 1490,[1] just about the time when "le pauvre petit escolier," François Villon, must have finished with the world and its troubles. In the historian of

"Le Grand Panurge et le païs
Des Papimanis ébahis,"

the force and individuality of the earlier poet had become the Gallic love of life, of health, strength, and splendour, which is the pre-eminent characteristic of Rabelais as it is of Balzac.[2] We shall hear now

[1] Life, by M. P. Jannet. *Œuvres Complètes de Rabelais* (ed. Jannet Picard). Other authorities give 1483 ; the date is uncertain.

[2] The best portrait of Rabelais I have seen is in the Bibliothèque Nationale at Paris—a cut by P. Taujé, 1739. Of earlier portraits that by N. Habert, 1699, is best.

and again of Rabelais later on, until Ronsard sings his epitaph in 1553, and a new school of literature begins very foreign in its methods to the cultured strength of the Curé de Meudon.

The statue looks towards a busy little square filled with a throng of traffickers, and crowded with gaily decorated booths: in the middle played the waters of a fountain circled by young acacia trees, and in their shade opened the inviting portals of the Hôtel de France. Only a Yorkshireman can do justice to a breakfast in Touraine; in Chinon the traditions of Panurge's friend, the famous "Innocent le Patissier," are evidently still kept up. We did our best, and were soon leisurely ascending the hill above which stretched the long broken line of the three fortresses whose ruins combine to form the relic of feudal strength known as Chinon. Arrived on the high ground, we passed beneath an iron lantern swung upon a rope across the road, and felt at once that we had left modern France behind us.

In front was the gateway of the castle with a mass of stone towering above it, crowned by a belfry at one corner with its aged, battered weathercock. Behind stretched the garlanded poles of countless vines peacefully growing within the walls of what was once the castle of the Plantagenets; to our right were various strange habitations scooped in the crumbled earth like the rock-dwellings on the road from Tours to Rochecorbon—strange juxtaposition of cavemen to feudal chatelaines. Like Pantagruel, we were half frightened at the "Caverne des Troglodytes." We might have heard the baying of a Cerberus. . . . No Bacbuc was there to throw us into a poetic frenzy, but the stones before us, eloquent in their ruin, were enough to rouse the dullest of imaginations. This cliff that rises steeply above the waters of the Vienne at some little distance from its banks was, like Amboise and Langeais, some four hundred years before Christ, the home of a Celtic tribe who drove out a still earlier race; traces of these latter are perhaps to be found in the dolmen of great stones about two miles to the east of Chinon, which may have marked the burial-place of a chief. In the writings of Gregory of Tours Chinon is described as a "castrum"—the word he always uses for a Roman fort, and the Romans left their traces here as they have done in nearly all the fortress cliffs which dominate the plains and rivers of Touraine; Roman funeral urns and the remains of bodies have been found that had been burnt *within* the ramparts, for the Roman Empire had, in 446 A.D., been shaken to its base by barbarian invasions; the Armorican Republic had just been joined by the men of Tours and Anjou, for whom a little later St. Mexme was performing miracles within the fort to keep at bay the forces of Aegidius. Soon after this must have begun to grow that mass of buildings which was still standing in

TOUR DE L'HORLOGE AND BRIDGE AT THE CHÂTEAU OF CHINON.

1793, and whose outlines a map of that date has preserved for us. The oldest remains of Gallo-Roman building are the enormous squared blocks of stone lying in the shrubberies a little farther on from the entrance and rather to the right. A sepulchral stone (still preserved within the château) was found among these remains of masonry, representing a man upright in a large tunic with wide sleeves; above it is the crescent-shaped sign so often found in monuments of this period.

Looking upwards at the whole line of buildings from the town, the arrangement of the three castles becomes apparent. Farthest to the right stood the castle and chapel of St. George, built by the Plantagenet kings to protect the one weak point in a position of almost unique strength and safety, the tongue of land to the east which unites the promontory on which the fortress rests to the line of hills beyond it. Joining these buildings, now levelled to the ground, to the Château du Milieu, is a fine stone bridge on bold archways with carved balustrades that leads to the drawbridge of the entrance beneath the Tour de l'Horloge. The little guardian in petticoats who replies to the traveller's summons for admission still hears him, and still answers his request, through the narrow slit cut in the thickness of the wall that communicates with the room in which the soldiers used to work the portcullis. Following the wall on the left we come to the first range of rooms, the suite of royal apartments opening out behind the high wall with the remains of chimneys at its various stages, which is all that is left of the great hall (on the first floor) where Jeanne d'Arc first met the King. Immediately behind this is the guardroom and armoury, next comes the kitchen, then the common living-room, whose windows are furnished with low stone seats on which to sit and watch the curve of the Vienne as it flows towards the Loire. From the next room, which has a small square bakehouse by its side, descends a strange little flight of steps through a narrow passage cut in the rock down to the bottom of the moat.

This moat is crossed by a stone bridge, which, like the longer one at the entrance, replaced the old wooden structure about the sixteenth century. It is defended by two towers ; from that on the left, built in the thirteenth century, perhaps the best view of the whole castle is to be obtained, while the full sweep of the river below is seen at its finest. The tower on the right is of the same epoch, and contains some of the best masonry in Chinon ; it was the old donjon of the castle, and its strong foundations plunge down into the moat beneath in one bold line of massive buttress. Within is a range of prisons, vault below vault, to the lowest level reached. We are now within the Fort du Coudray, the last of the three castles, at the extreme western edge of the cliff; its chief feature is the fine Tour du Moulin, where the mill of the fortress once stood, whose pointed leaden roof and widespread sails must have been a strange feature in the old castle. Along the wall of which this tower forms the western corner are the oldest relics of the twelfth-century buildings.

Chinon more than all other places in this part of the country leaves an impression of antiquity far greater than that of its neighbours; it is easy to people Blois with the gallants of Henry III.'s Court, or the intrigues of Louis XIV.; Chenonceaux tells its own light, uneventful story in every ripple of reflected sunbeam upon its graceful windows; but Chinon, greater in extent than all of them, a very wilderness of towers and battlements—Chinon is in ruins irretrievably. It would seem as if the movements to which its walls gave birth were too weighty for the nurse that bore them, and the mother of so many royal fortunes has not had strength to live to see the fulness of their destiny. The history of the Plantagenets of Chinon has passed on to the walls of Windsor.

The dense woodland of larches, oaks, and firs which stretches to the north-east, almost to the valley of the Indre, was no doubt one of the attractions of Chinon to Fulk Nerra and to the greatest of his descendants, Henry II. of England and Anjou, whose favourite home in France was here. It remains for us to complete the story of the Angevin kings which was traced up to the highest point of their prosperity. A great change is now to come. With the death of "the young King," his son Henry, in 1183, discord at once broke out between Richard, Geoffrey, and John, the other three sons; a further element of complication was introduced by the death of Geoffrey of Brittany, whose son Arthur was almost immediately claimed by the French King as his ward. The confusion had reached such a pitch that Richard had seized his father's treasury at Chinon, when news came of the great Saracen victory over Guy of Lusignan, which gave Jerusalem itself into the hands of the Infidels, and Richard took the cross from the Archbishop of Tours.

The would-be Crusaders began operations against the Infidel by quarrelling among themselves at home; amidst a general disorder Richard joined Philip of France against his father, and Henry II., hotly besieged within Le Mans, had but just time to escape from the flaming town towards the Norman frontier. Suddenly changing his direction, in a ride that equalled the legendary rush of the Black Falcon on Saumur, the King spurred frenziedly back to Chinon, while his attendant knights fainted or died from fatigue and wounds upon the way. Then Philip advanced by Chaumont and Amboise as far as Rochecorbon, and proposed a meeting at Azay;

but the devil which had helped Fulk Nerra on his ride had entered into Henry after his escape from Maine, a devil of despair and pain that racked his peace of mind while it tortured his body with a fever. Tours fell to the French King, and Henry was unable to move from his room. Then he was summoned again to meet Philip at Colombières between Azay and Tours. By a great effort Henry started from Chinon, and rested on his way at the Commanderie of the Knights Templars at Ballan; there, leaning for support in his extreme anguish against a wall, he was persuaded to rest for a while by William the Marshal. The meeting was for the next day, and neither his own son nor the French King would put it off. On that July morning two great shocks of thunder from a clear sky put the finishing touch to the collapse of the poor King, who was obliged to be held fainting upon his horse —he signed a humiliating peace.

On his return to Chinon he had just strength left to soundly rate the monks of Canterbury, who had come at this inopportune moment to present their demands; one of them, as he went out, cursed him by the memory of the murdered Becket. That night his Chancellor was reading to him the list of the rebels. "Sire," said he, "may Jesus Christ help me! the first name which is written here is the name of Count John, your son." Then Henry turned his face to the wall, caring no more for himself or for the world. For some days he lay half unconscious, muttering, "Shame, shame on a conquered King." At last he was carried out to die before the altar of the castle chapel. The servants stripped his body and laid it naked on the ground to be covered by a cloak borrowed from William de Trihan. The last rites were with difficulty arranged by William the Marshal. "Robed as for coronation, with a crown of gold upon his head, a gold ring upon his finger, sandals upon his feet, and a sceptre in his gloved right hand," he was borne across the bridge that he had built to be laid in state in the Abbey Church of Fontevrault; thither came his unworthy son Richard to see the body, which streamed with blood, it is said, as he approached it. Henry was buried before the high altar by Bartholomew the Archbishop of Tours, in July 1189.

Three years afterwards Philip of France, returned from the Crusades, was ravaging Anjou. The attacks on the foreign dominions of England which had been prompted by the news of Richard's imprisonment ceased for the moment when he was released. But in 1193 the attacks upon Touraine had become so fierce and systematic that Richard left England never to return, and made direct for Tours, where he drove out the canons of St. Martin as being friends of the French King. He then blockaded Loches and took it, turned on Blois, and surprised so many valuable papers and cases that Philip was obliged to make a truce; finally, where the Seine bends suddenly to the north, Richard built his famous Château Gaillard with its three lines of defence very much like the walls of Chinon. The fame of the Lionheart, which gains little from his doings in French territory, is still less increased by the story of his death. In 1199, being very much pressed by want of money, he suddenly heard that a treasure had been discovered at Chalus, and claimed it as the overlord. In attempting to take the castle he was shot, and died from the mortification of the wound.[1]

John, who had been appointed as his brother's heir, hurried to Chinon and was acknowledged King by the royal household. But a counter-claimant appeared in Arthur of Bretagne, who was at Tours with his mother, Constance, supported by the King of France and the adherence of the barons of Touraine. To attempt to foil Constance, Eleanor came out from Fontevrault and took up her son John's cause. A peace was patched up by the Dauphin's marriage with Blanche, niece of the English King. In the next year John, having put away his first wife Avice of Gloucester, scandalised the barons by his marriage with Isabel, the daughter of the Count of Angoulême, and spent the next summer at Chinon with her and Berengaria the widow of his brother Richard.

[1] In the *Chroniques de Normandie*, a MS. of the fifteenth century, there is a strange picture of the storming of Chalus, showing Richard's wound in the shoulder.

Discontent grew more and more throughout the provinces. Already had John been sentenced by default to lose his lands and fiefs, when Philip in 1201 attacked Arques while Arthur of Brittany besieged Tours, where his small band of knights was reinforced by Hugh de la Marche (the bridegroom John had first insulted) and by Geoffrey of Lusignan, an inveterate foe of the Plantagenets. The next move was to the siege of Mirebeau, whither John's mother Eleanor had gone after her second retreat to Fontevrault. Arthur was taken prisoner by the relieving forces which John brought up, sent to Falaise, and was no more heard of. This was a fatal mistake, for it drove John's rebellious subjects to choose between him and Philip. Their choice was soon made. By spring of the next year the taking of the Château Gaillard drove the English from all French lands north of the Loire; on Midsummer Eve, 1205, after a long and desperate siege, Chinon was taken too, and by the beginning of 1206 the English were finally driven out of France.

In the thirteenth century there was not much of importance that happened at Chinon. The French monarchy, so much enlarged and strengthened by Philip Augustus, was still further expanded by the religion and the higher life of St. Louis, "the most loyal man of his age," whom Charles VIII. and all France of the time looked back upon as their patron saint, and with whom died the last spark of the crusading spirit.

In 1309 occurred one of the few notable events of the next century at Chinon, the examination of Jacques Molay, Grand Master of the Knights Templars, by the Pope's cardinals in state assembled. The order of the Templars had been founded nearly two hundred years before by nine knights who defended the Temple at Jerusalem. Growing in wealth and strength, the Knights had left Palestine and built their Temple opposite the Louvre in Paris. Strange rumours of the wealth and wickedness of this secret society were rife throughout France, and suddenly the King seized every member of it; the "Procès des Templiers"[1] gives some horrible details of their trial and examination. Meanwhile the Pope,

[1] In the collection of *Documents inédits sur l'histoire de France*. See also *Revue des deux Mondes*, 15th Jan. 1891, "Le Procès des Templiers d'après des documents nouveaux," Ch. V. Langlois; and L. Delisle, *Mémoires sur les opérations financières des Templiers*. The Knights Templars so unrighteously condemned six centuries ago have only quite lately received the justice due to them; the verdict of Michelet must be reversed in the face of the later facts forthcoming. It seems clear that the chief, if not the only reason for the summary destruction of the order was to be found in the rapacity and indebtedness of the King. From the acknowledged safety of their fortresses in Europe it had resulted that the Templars became the bankers of the warriors and prelates of the troublous times of the Crusades. The wide extent of their connections enabled them to begin operations of the highest value with the Jews and Lombards, and their inevitable rise in power and importance was the beginning of their unpopularity. The King who hunted them down was also their heaviest creditor. The only testimony against them was the confessions wrung from the anguish of the prisoners by the torture to which they were mercilessly condemned.

who was in "Babylonish captivity" at Avignon, was made to dissolve their order, many Templars (including the Grand Master) were burnt in Paris, and almost the only remnant of their existence left in France is the name of "Commanderie," which still clings, as at Ballan, to the places where once a house of the famous order used to stand. This particular Commanderie, whose graceful modern rooms are grouped round the little library with its carved ceiling, which is the last relic of the Templars, was inhabited even down to 1790 by the Knights of St. John, who succeeded the old order.

In 1337 began the Hundred Years' War, the struggle between France and England for the mastery which began with the crushing defeats of Crécy and Poitiers. Then came the period of Du Guesclin's victories over the English from 1360 to 1380, only to be followed by another twenty years of disaster which ended in the catastrophe of Agincourt. The fortunes of France were indeed at a low ebb; it is from Chinon that the first ray of hope appears; the short visit of Joan of Arc, the beginning of that romantic and inexplicable episode of which she is the heroine, is the salient point among all the traditions of the castle. The years that immediately followed Agincourt were terrible years for France. The Dukes of Bourbon and Orleans, fighting in the front rank, had been taken prisoner, and the power of the Armagnac party was still further weakened by the alliance of the Queen (who had been exiled to Tours for her misconduct) with the Burgundian party. The massacres in Paris which followed resulted in the death of some two thousand of the Armagnacs, and the Dauphin himself hardly escaped with life. The so-called "Cabochiens" were filling Paris with bloodshed and disorder.[1] Soon after the death of Henry of England the poor French King ceased the mockery of life that still remained to him; the touching attachment of his people to this crazed monarch would alone show how oppressive was the rule of the princes who were now in power. In 1422 the Dauphin assumed his royal robes as Charles VII. in Berri, while Bedford and his Englishmen in Paris were shouting "Long live the King of France and England" round the little son of Henry V.

The English had run a wedge into the very heart of France from the sea-coast to Paris, and to this lazy, kindly, good-looking Charles VII. was left the task of turning them out. His defeats at the very outset were so numerous that he was nicknamed "Le Roi de Bourges," and the misery of France went on unabated.[2] The state of the people at this time

[1] Monstrelet relates the entry of the Burgundians into Paris on 28th May 1418, and the *Journal of the Bourgeois de Paris* gives terrible details of the scenes in the streets during the continual massacres that went on. He describes especially the horrors of Sunday, 29th May, in that year, when the dead "étaient en tas comme porcs au milieu de la boue," beneath the splashing of the ceaseless raindrops.

[2] The *Grandes Chroniques* give a fearful picture of these miseries.

was frightful ; wolves were fighting for the corpses of the dead in the churchyards of Paris, churches were sacked, castles burnt to the ground, the lands left untilled, a hideous "danse Macabre" among the tombs came into fashion, wild rumours of portents and prodigies were in the air, when in 1423 the King came to Chinon with the Queen of Sicily and the Duc d'Alençon to assemble the States-General, to deliberate with his small Court over the small part of France that had been left him by the English, and to receive the Count of Richemont, Arthur of Bretagne, who had offered his services against the enemy.

The evil influences of La Trémouille and the anti-nationalist party had already begun to be felt in this as in other matters about the Court, when in 1428 letters came from Tours praying for help against the English at Orleans, the northernmost point of the Loire and the key to Southern France, which was besieged by Bedford.

The Court was full of bickerings and jealousies, and the treasury was empty, but the States voted

In eighteen months more than 1500 men had died in Paris. Some monks of St. Denis, seeing men and women dancing to the sound of music in a certain town, asked why they did so. "Nous avons vu nos voisins morts, et les voyons de jour en jour mourir," and they danced for joy that their time had not yet come. That evening the greater part were dead or dying. The actual horrors of the time were reflected in a corruption of morality and dissoluteness of manners which gave the graver chroniclers small cause to wonder that God was chastening France by means of his scourge the King of England.

subsidies, and in the next year help came from unexpected quarters. The King was in fact very little worthy of the veneration by which that help was inspired, when in the midst of the intrigue and idleness of his Court appeared the strange figure of the peasant girl from Domremy.

## CHAPTER IV

### CHINON (*Continued*)

"La Royne Blanche comme ung lys
Qui chantoit à voix de sereine,
Berthe au grand pied, Bietris, Allys;
Harembourges, qui tint le Mayne,
Et Jehanne la bonne Lorraine
Qu' Anglois bruslèrent à Rouen;
Où sont-ilz, Vierge Souveraine?
Mais où sont les neiges d'antan?"—VILLON.

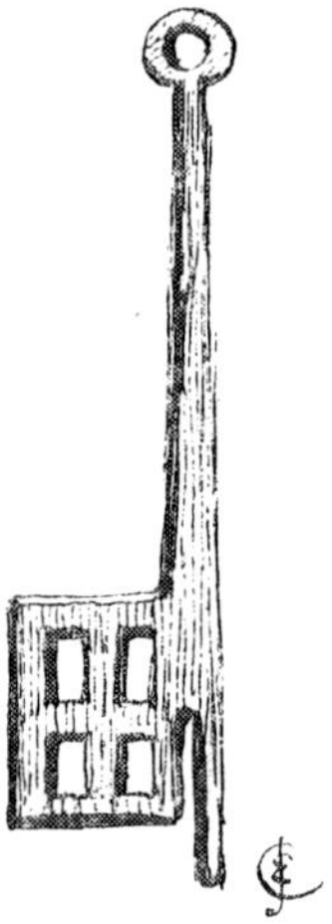

FOURTEENTH-CENTURY KEY (from the Collection of M. Lacoste, Rue des Saints Pères, Paris).

ON Sunday, 6th March 1429, Jeanne d'Arc came to Chinon, and the well is still shown where she alighted off her horse, and the house of the "bonne femme" who sheltered her. Once within the château she was lodged within the Tour du Coudray until the young King should find time to rouse himself from the caresses of Aloyse de Castelnau and give audience to the peasant girl about whom his courtiers were already disputing.

The introduction to the royal presence, hard enough already for Jeanne, was made still harder by the indifference of that King who had been the ideal of her dreams, by the studied insolence and opposition of his counsellors, and by the whisperings of a licentious Court. She needed all her courage to support the cold and cynical reception which was all she found in return for enthusiasm and offers of victory ; and the Chapel of St. Martin in the castle precincts must have witnessed no slight struggle between her reluctance to go forward and her eagerness to fulfil her destiny. The contemptuous trial of her powers made by the King at her very first appearance, the examinations and tests which she was afterwards to undergo, the numberless perils of her position, all must have combined to make her self-sought trial wellnigh harder than she could bear. But "aide toi et le ciel t'aidera" was her unflinching motto, and to the taunting questions of the officers she would only answer, "Les hommes d'armes batailleront et Dieu donnera la victoire." Of her personal appearance scarcely a word has come down to us ; that she had long black hair, that after a little practice she could sit a horse in full armour as bravely as the rest, that her chief charm lay in the firm accents of her soft low voice, such are almost the only hints we have of the personality of Jeanne d'Arc.[1]

[1] See in Beaucourt, *Hist. de Charles VII.* vol. ii. p. 218, "Lettre de Guy et d'André de Laval aux dames de Lavale." "Ladite Pucelle me fit très bon visage à mon frère et à moi. Elle était armée de toutes pièces, sauf la tête, et tenait sa lance en mains . . . elle fit venir du

Whatever may have actually happened during the period of uncertainty and doubt while she was kept within the castle, some weeks later she left Chinon for Tours clad in complete armour with her followers beside her, and encouraged at last by the full confidence of the King.[1] It does not belong to the story of Chinon to describe how she left Tours for Blois and so to Orleans, where she conquered the enemy as she had promised ; how she led the King to his coronation at Rheims ; how later on she fell by treachery, the only foe she ever feared, into English hands, and was burnt at the stake in the market-place of Rouen.

There is no fact more astonishing in history and none better established than this episode of Joan of Arc.[2] She was not believed in by many of those in power in her time, a time which was still strongly imbued with the principles of feudalism and keenly suspicious of movements in a new direction ; in her

vin et me dit qu'elle m'en ferait bientôt boire à Paris. Ce semble chose toute divine de son fait, de la voir et de l'ouïr. . . . Puis se tournant sur la porte de l'église, qui était bien proche, elle dit d'une assez douce voix de femme : 'Vous, les prêtres et gens d'Église, faites processions et prières à Dieu.' "

At Orleans there is some early fifteenth-century German tapestry showing the entry of Jeanne d'Arc into Chinon. The castle is an impossibility of needlework, but the Maid herself is represented much as she is described by the letters of the Lavals.

[1] See Monstrelet, *Chroniques*, II. lvii.

[2] Quicherat's five volumes, which contain both the "procès de condamnation," and the "procès de réhabilitation" which somewhat tardily followed it, present the best contemporary authorities for the facts.

were personified ideas pre-eminently in advance of her age; that intense "amour de Patrie," which becomes a worship of the idea of Nationality, was as foreign to feudal society as was the doctrine of liberty of conscience; both of these ideas were expressed in the movement led by the peasant girl, and both are arguments as strongly favourable in a later democratic society as they were prejudicial to her in the aristocracy of Church and State in her own time. "Il y a ès livres de nostre Seigneur plus que ès vostres," she says in the examination before the ecclesiastics ordered by the King, and the bishops found indeed that there were more things in heaven and earth than had been dreamt of in their philosophy.

If there is anything more strange than the silence of France while her heroine was being tried by unjust judges and cruelly done to death, it is the almost complete silence, either for praise or blame,[1] which for a long time follows the burning of the Maid at Rouen; but of later years all France seems to have suddenly waxed enthusiastic over this episode in her history; statues, dramas, poems have followed one another in quick succession; it needed the Revolution and the rise of the people to exalt the shepherdess into a national saint. "I never

[1] If we except the "procès de réhabilitation," and *Le Mistère du Siège d'Orleans* (produced in 1467), which ends before her death, we can find nothing worth the writing about Jeanne d'Arc till far later times.

committed the crime," says Southey, "of reading Voltaire's *La Pucelle*," and we recommend our readers to follow the English poet's example; the untrue picture given of the Maid of Orleans by Shakespeare becomes in the later work a cynically false and distorted libel. M. Joseph Fabre, whose enthusiastic work is one of the most conscientious monographs existing on this subject, draws out a strange parallel between Joan of Arc and Socrates with regard to the visions and voices which the shepherdess constantly affirmed had been vouchsafed to her. The results of later investigations go to show that at the time of Jeanne's visions, St. Michael, on whose assistance she lays especial stress, was particularly in the minds of all devout Frenchmen. The hated English had just received a decisive check among the swirling tides and treacherous quicksands of the rock of Mont St. Michel, on the northern coasts; the patron saint of that strange island fortress seemed to have already begun his defence of French territory.

But such supernatural problems are too wide for us; more interesting is it to trace the gradual rehabilitation of Joan of Arc in the good opinion of the English, her first and unfair judges.[1] In that opinion she passed through all the stages of the sorceress, the heroine, and the saint. While the

[1] See on this point a brilliant article by M. James Darmesteter published in *La Nouvelle Revue*.

first rumours of her presence were still rife in the English camp,[1] came her brief and emphatic letter: ' Allez-vous-en en votre pays, de par Dieu. Roi d'Angleterre, si vous n'obéissez, sachez qu'en quelque lieu de France que j'atteigne vos gens, je les en ferai sortir bon gré mal gré." And if the English soldiers thought they had the powers of hell to deal with, they found them no less hard to overcome than any heavenly help. "The Lord had put a sword into her mouth," and even Germany and Italy had recognised its power.

There is no contemporary mention of her in English writings, except a line in William of Worcester. Caxton gives a small page to her in his English Chronicles, in which is mentioned the lie that Shakespeare has preserved against her tainted purity. Historians, whose chief profession was the faith of Christ born in a manger, were equally unfavourable in dealing with the peasant heroine of France.[2] By Thomas Fuller she is still classed with the Witch of Endor, and it is only in the eighteenth century that the change begins. Then only, when France was "too advanced to believe in God, and not advanced enough to believe in the Divine," the Rationalism of England said that Jeanne was at least not of hell. As Quicherat forty years ago first

[1] See *Journal d'un Bourgeois de Paris*, année 1429.

[2] In Holinshed, ed. 1577, she is called "that monstrous maid, Jean la Pucell de Dieu."

showed her truly to the world, amidst the horror of the courtiers and ecclesiastics of her time at the flood of faith and purity and truth she poured out upon the miserable pettiness of their depraved ambitions, so Guthrie in 1747 first pointed out how the least tint of falsehood would have smirched her fame, and how she came out pure as fine gold from every proof. The truth had come at last, and from the most convincing quarter—from the country that had least to win in proving it. To Southey she is the one pure figure in a luxurious and selfish age; to Carlyle these "French without heart, mockers forgetting God, are not worthy of this noble virgin," this maid "to whom all maidens upon earth should bend," as Landor bids them.

After Jeanne's death a certain change seems to have come over the King's life at Chinon.[1] From the Tour d'Argentan, in the corner of the Château du Milieu farthest from the entrance, it is said that a secret passage used to wind,[2] by which Charles VII., at that time more worthy of the name of King, visited Agnes Sorel, whose statue rests upon its sculptured lambs at Loches.

"Je vais combattre ; Agnès l'ordonne ;
Adieu repos ; plaisirs adieu,"

[1] The fame of the favourite of Charles VII. has rather obscured the virtue and goodness of his wife, who quietly encouraged all the best influences of the time; see the miniature in *Les Douze Perilz d'Enfer* by her learned chaplain Robert Blondel, in which he presents the book to her, 1455.—*Biblioth. de l'Arsenal.*

[2] No traces of it exist now.

as Béranger makes him say, and whether owing to the influence of "la belle des belles" or not, the King of 1450 is a very different man from the "roi fainéant" for whom Jeanne d'Arc died.

> "Dunois, la Tremouille, Saintrailles,
> O Français ! quel jour enchanté
> Quand des lauriers de vingt batailles
> Je couronnerai ta beauté !
> Français, nous devrons à ma belle
> Moi la gloire et vous le bonheur.
> J'oubliais l'honneur auprès d'elle ;
> Agnès me rend tout à l'honneur." [1]

The changed King had turned out his old favourites and replaced them by men like the Count de Richemont and Jacques Cœur ; [2] by 1453, after the death of Talbot in Guienne, there were no more English in France except at Calais. In that same year

[1] The lines of Colonel Lovelace come irresistibly into our memory with their higher thought—

> "I could not love thee, dear, so much,
> Loved I not honour more."

[2] Jacques Cœur was "argentier d'iceluy roy de France" (Charles VII.), says Du Clerq, "lequel Jacques Cœur estoit extrait de petite génération sans quelque noblesse. En sa jeunesse il se bouta en marchandise . . . et devint sy puissant par tous les royaulmes qu'il expédioit et même comme on disoit en Sarragie. Il avait fait faire à Bourges une maison la plus riche de quoy on pouvait parler." This house with its motto "à cœur vaillant rien impossible" is well worth seeing ; it has been charmingly described by Mr. Henry James.

Jacques Cœur when exiled from the French Court was received with great consideration at Rome, and though he had been fined ten million crowns, yet found enough left to live as honourably as he had done before. He never returned to France. See Thomas Basin, *Histoire de Charles VII. et Louis XI.*, iv. 26, also Du Clerq, *Mémoires*, III. iii., and Mathieu de Coucy, *Chroniques*, cix.

Constantinople had been taken by the Turks, and the learning of the Eastern capital was scattered broadcast in the west to grow into the full flower of the Renaissance.

But even Agnes Sorel could not charm away the troubles which pursued Charles VII. in all his châteaux. At Chinon the Dauphin had been whispering with the Sire de Chabannes, and from the window of his rooms was plotting away the honour of the Scottish guards. Useless to execute several of the soldiers and to expel the Dauphin—one trouble was but followed by another. Heralds arrived with their futile explanations and were sent back in anger, and at last the King with his soldiers wearily set out for Amboise on his way northwards. At Méhun sur Yèvre he died, and the news soon came to Marie d'Anjou, the wife he had left at home, that she was a widow, for black care sat behind the horseman and killed him more surely than the arrows of the enemy.[1]

The reign of Louis XI. was marked at Chinon by the arrival at the royal stronghold of Margaret of Anjou. Quitting for a time the struggles between Lancaster and York, this somewhat turbulent Queen had left Kirkcudbright for Brittany and Anjou to get help from Louis XI., who promised more than might have been expected of him. He probably had his reasons. He had already helped René, and the house

[1] 22d July 1461; see Mathieu de Coucy, *Chroniques*, cap. cxxv.

of Anjou must be still further conciliated by the help of René's daughter. Any diversion, too, that would tend to unsettle the dynasty in England was a welcome aid, keeping the English in a state of enforced neutrality; there was even the chance of Calais being surrendered as the price of help. So, strangely enough, Peter de Brézé, the Seneschal of Normandy, was offered his choice of continued prison or the chances of the English wars, and we find him later on assisting the restless Margaret at the siege of Alnwick, while the strife between the two parties went on as fiercely as ever.

Louis himself did not often darken Chinon with his presence. It was close to here, at Les Forges, in the forest to the north-east, that while the King was at dinner, "luy vint comme une perclusion," and he lost the power of speech. Commines, who tells us of the scene, was sent for, and waited on his sick master for forty days. Other courtiers, who had not been so well advised in their offers of assistance, were exiled from the Court as soon as Louis recovered. His great fear was a loss of authority in his weakness. All the time of his illness the two brothers, Louis and Charles d'Amboise, were writing despatches and arranging affairs of State in a lower room, but every letter had to be taken up to the paralytic, who could barely see or speak, to receive the mockery of his approval. It was at the time of his recovery from this attack that he at last released

Cardinal Balue, whom he kept imprisoned fourteen years. His last and fatal illness overtook him at Plessis-lez-Tours.

A more interesting event is the betrothal of Philippe de Commines to Mdlle. de Montsoreau, which took place at Chinon in 1473. It was during the strange scene at Peronne, where the craft of Louis almost overreached itself and placed him in the hands of Charles, Duke of Burgundy, that Commines had first learned the extraordinary intellectual powers of Louis XI., with which he seems to have been so much dazzled that he lost sight of the depravity of that odious monarch's real character. Just before his betrothal the historian had passed into France, where "Louis XI. lui fit cet honneur de dire qu'il l'avait bien servy à Peronne." The Duke of Burgundy let him off all debts on his estate, the convenient sum of 6000 livres came in from a jeweller at Tours, and he was richly rewarded by the French King for a loyalty which was frequently held up to the imitation of his companions. That there was a real tie of sympathy and friendship between these two very different characters is seen, if in nothing else, in the fact that Commines was almost the only man who could understand the King's enfeebled utterances during his illness. This keenness of temperament was reflected, too, in the finesse with which he managed all the political affairs with which he was entrusted either in France or Italy.

Among his other rewards he was made Governor of Chinon in 1476, and soon began to take that active part in politics which ended later on in his imprisonment at Loches by Anne of Beaujeu, who held the royal power for her young brother Charles VIII. "I have ventured on the great ocean," he says regretfully, "and the waves devoured me." But he emerged with safety later on, and the world gained his history, written, it is said, in the hours of his enforced leisure. He was employed by Charles VIII. and favoured by Louis XII., though this latter monarch showed him some little ingratitude, and perhaps rather feared the political experience of a minister of Louis XI. His work as an ambassador, especially in Italy, was always of service to his country; his work as a writer was the only thing of the kind that could have been compared to that of Machiavelli or even of Guicciardini, the first sound attempt at a philosophy of history; and by his death at Argenton, near Chinon, France lost one of her most skilful statesmen and far the best historian of his time.[1]

[1] Montaigne's opinion of Commines is worth recording here. "En Monsieur Philippe de Commines il y a cecy : vous y trouverez le langage doux et agréable d'une naifve simplicité, la narration pure, et en laquelle *la bonne foy* de l'autheur reluit evidamment exempte de vanité parlant de soy, et d'affection et d'envie parlant d'autruy." Montaigne's recommendation of his own essays to his readers could produce no better justification for an author's work. Matthieu d'Arras, a

> "Si tu n'as plus que faire en cette église ici,"

says Ronsard, in some lines on Commines,

> "Retourne en ta maison et conte à ton fils comme
> Tu as vu le tombeau du premier gentilhomme
> Qui d'un cœur vertueux fit à la France voir
> Que c'est honneur de joindre aux armes le sçavoir."

It is from the Italy that was the scene of Commines' most brilliant negotiations that the next actor comes who plays an important part at Chinon. In 1498 Louis XII., who had just come to the throne, was applying to Pope Alexander VI. for a divorce from his first wife, Jeanne de France. The royal letters came to the Vatican during the reign of the Borgias. Lucrezia was being given in marriage to one after another of the Italian princes as it suited the policy of her unscrupulous father. Cæsar Borgia, who had not long before murdered his brother, the Duke of Gandia, was longing to give full rein to his ambition, to throw away his Cardinal's hat and take up the sword, to fight his way from a successful captaincy to the Dukedom of the Romagna, and even higher honours. The request of Louis XII. came at a very opportune moment. The bill of divorce was easily bought from Cæsar's father by the gift of the Duchy of Valentinois to his son, and a treaty promising equal advantages to France and

friend of Commines, tells us he was tall and handsome, that he spoke German, Italian, and Spanish, that his memory was prodigious, and his industry amazing.

the Vatican. In the general interchange of civilities Georges d'Amboise was given a Cardinal's hat, and

CÆSAR BORGIA (drawn from the Woodcut in Paulus Jovius, ed. 1575).

towards the end of 1498 Cæsar Borgia set out from Ostia for Marseilles, accompanied by the Baron de

Traus, the French ambassador, and provided with ample funds for his lavish expenditure upon the way from the two hundred thousand ducats seized from the unfortunate Bishop of Calahorra.

In those days the science of etiquette was very fearfully and wonderfully arranged, and in all their treatises the worried officials at the French Court could find no mention of the reception proper to a Pope's son. The difficulty was evaded without suppressing the gorgeous entry which it was well known the Italian had prepared for himself and his suite. The King went hunting with his Court and met Borgia some miles outside the town; upon the bridge across the river the Cardinal de Rohan was ready to receive the Italians, and headed the procession that started for the castle gates; every detail of its magnificence has been carefully preserved for us.

First came eighty mules in gorgeous harness blazoned with Cæsar Borgia's crest and arms, followed by the finest horses of the prince's stables; then eighteen pages riding, clad in "velours cramoisie," two of them resplendent in cloth of gold; more mules followed "still more exquisitely appointed," evidently carrying "the precious documents from Rome," thought the onlookers; after, amid a flourish of drums and trumpets, rode the new Duc de Valentinois and his suite, among whom was the Cardinal d'Amboise. The duke was resplendent in red satin and cloth of gold, and thickly covered with jewels; great rubies were in his cap, his very boots were sewn with precious stones.[1] A crowd of mules, carriages, and litters closed the procession;

> "Ainsi entra pour avoir grand renom
> Ledit Seigneur au Château de Chinon,"

sings the poet whom Brantôme copied; but while the formal welcome was in progress within the royal apartments, the old soldiers who had fought through Italy with Charles VIII. were laughing at this new-fledged Frenchman's ostentation, a display, by the way, which Cæsar rarely allowed himself in Italy.

That evening the articles of the treaty were agreed upon—the divorce was granted and the alliance formed against Naples; in return, France was to help the Pope in the Romagna, Cæsar was to receive the Duchy of Valentinois and certain sums down in ready money; better than all, he was to be given the services of one hundred French knights; the *fleurs de lys* of France were to be quartered with the Borgia arms—"c'était lui livrer l'Italie," says Michelet. But what was perhaps nearer to the duke's

[1] An authentic portrait of Cæsar Borgia is a difficult thing to find. Of the portraits in the Bibliothèque Nationale, a drawing by Lecœur is the best, which is probably taken from the woodcut in Paulus Jovius. The famous description of Cæsar Borgia which Jovius gives is worth inserting: "Faciem atro rubore suffusam . . . oculosque introrsus recedentes, et atroci vipereoque obtutu scintillantes ac igneos ostenderet, quos nec amici quidem et familiares contuendo ferre possent; quanquam eos inter foeminas jocabundus, mira commutatione ad lenitatem convertere consuesset."—PAULI JOVII, *Elogia*, p. 201. 1575.

ambition, the promise of a high alliance, was not so easily performed : negotiations dragged on unwillingly, and when the Court left for Loches in the spring Cæsar was half inclined to return to Italy in disgust ; but he stayed a little longer, and at Blois we shall hear how he fared.

The later history of Chinon is not so full of interest ; the movement of events passes to the other châteaux, whose Renaissance windows had been scarcely thought of when Cæsar Borgia was in France. The castle is somewhat troubled by the vicissitudes of the Wars of Religion and frequently changes hands, not without suffering from the excesses of both parties. The townspeople of Chinon, who seem to have shown an extraordinary amount of pluck and spirit in these trying times, were still further harassed by a terrible visitation of the plague: the first attack lasted four years. After the murder of Guise at Blois had still further embittered party spirit throughout the kingdom, and Henry of Navarre had led his forces to Chinon on his way to attack the Duc de Mayenne, who had succeeded his murdered brother in the headship of the Catholic League, the plague broke out again in 1589, and throughout the unhappy little town the red and white crosses were marked upon the doors, and great fires burnt at every thirty paces to purify the poisoned air. A strange glimpse of the habits of the time is given in the records of the rude sanitary precautions that were taken at this crisis: "pourceaux, vaches, pigeons, oies, cannes, ou autres bêtes immondes" are to be kept out of the houses, says the edict, which might have been framed for the benefit of a benighted Irish peasantry; one Matthieu Renard and his wife are charged with the care of the sick at a fixed price.

In the midst of all this distress events outside were following fast. The letter of Henri III. to his wife Louise, at Chinon, reached her after her husband's death by the knife of Jacques Clément; she retired to an inconsolable widowhood in Chenonceaux. The old Cardinal de Bourbon had been summoned from his prison in the castle to dispute his royal title with Henry of Navarre, and died without defending it. Chinon was rapidly entering on the last century of its existence.

The history of the town in the first years of the seventeenth century gains considerably in interest from the careful accounts of its "Receveur, M. Besnard," which have been preserved by M. de Cougny. After the peace this good M. Besnard, whose acquaintance it is quite worth while to make in these records, welcomes with his fellow-townsmen the Prince of Condé. He fires salvos of honour from certain "fauconnaux" placed upon the bridge, which was still in ruins, and presents the traditional offering of fruit and wine, nay, even searches for artichokes to send up to the castle, and "confitures sèches" for the princess — the last refinement of politeness.

Condé was soon sent off to Vincennes, and there was no one now to send sweetmeats to the ladies, for Rochefort, the "âme damnée" of the Cardinal, is there instead, and soon the whole town is cringing to the great Richelieu himself in the full pride of that despotism which was partly forced upon him by the anarchy of Huguenot revolutions. How the delicate but frugal soul of Besnard would have shuddered had he seen the town-clerk of a community grown recklessly extravagant spend nearly three hundred livres upon a single fête. But it was almost the last that Chinon, either town or castle, was to see. In 1628 the outraged inhabitants with difficulty persuaded Muret, the King's architect, to spare their castle walls; and when Chinon was joined with Langeais, Richelieu, and other estates to the great possessions of the Cardinal, the old castle only bored him, and was designedly left to ruin and decay.

One of the greatest of the feudal monuments was allowed to moulder into uselessness, like the institutions of which it was a remnant, by the man with whose name is chiefly connected the final crushing of the feudal spirit. M. Touchard Lafosse says that in 1758 the room where Jeanne d'Arc was received still stood in its entirety. He publishes, too,[1]

[1] Paris, Delahays, 1856, *La Loire Historique*.

an engraving that shows the complete lines of the fortress before the château of the Plantagenets had fallen; but for two centuries the whole castle has been slowly crumbling to its foundations, and it will probably take many more before time has utterly destroyed its mighty buttresses and walls. The stones of Chinon will die hard, but its memories will live, though both are growing older, and perhaps weaker, year by year.

# CHAPTER V

## FONTEVRAULT

"Think how many royal bones
Sleep within these heaps of stones. . . .
Here's a world of pomp and state
Buried in dust, once dead by fate."

F. BEAUMONT.

ON a cold winter's morning we started from Chinon to follow that funeral procession of the Plantagenets, which we had pictured to ourselves before, to their last home at Fontevrault.

The road leads straight southward from the town for a short distance away from the Vienne, then turning sharply to the west and north winds through pleasant apple orchards and walnut-trees till it joins the river bank again opposite Port Guyot. Some three or four miles farther on we reached the extreme limit of the Province of Indre et Loire, the town of Candes,[1] where the dark and swift waters of the Vienne mingled with the ice-bound current of the Loire. The bright rays of a December

[1] M. Touchard Lafosse (*op. cit.*) publishes a very good engraving of the view of Candes from the right bank of the Vienne.

sun lit up the circles of broken ice that were swirled rapidly down the stream, and touched the tall sails of the black windmills dark against the sky-line of the western shore, where numbers of little churches between the forest and the river marked the sites of villages and castles long since in ruins. And Candes itself is little like to what it was. Placed at the meeting of the waters, it must very early have been marked out as a place of some importance, and indeed, before 400 there must have been a considerable number of clergy at the church which the famous Bishop of Tours had built here, for in that year St. Martin, being on a visit to the priests, died at Candes.[1] His body was, after some dispute with the men of Poitou, buried at Tours, and the church at Candes was consecrated afresh to his memory. It was no unworthy companion, on a small scale, to that great shrine at Tours, of which but two towers remain to indicate its ancient size and beauty.

In any other country than Touraine such a church as that at Candes would have alone made the district famous, and no greater surprise had encountered us than this sudden sight of sculptured saints and battlemented roofs[2] at an opening of the twisting little

[1] In 1495 the town had already begun to decrease in size and importance. See Commines, VIII. iv., "La ville (Vigevano) ne vaut poinct Sainct Martin de Cande, qui n'est riens."

[2] This combination of church and fortress was not uncommon in the Middle Ages, and was not without its value. The Cathedral of Nar-

village street. The exterior decoration of the porch, which is flanked by two towers crowned with machicolations like a fortress, shows signs of the double influences at work during the century when the church was built. The date in the nave is 1215, when it was probably begun ; it was finished towards the end of the century, and the sculpture of the figures round the porch, though terribly mutilated, shows signs of the older Byzantine tendencies slowly yielding to the new Gothic art. The fourteen statues rest on a base richly decorated with foliage and strange monsters, twisting round the heads of kings and queens carved with marvellous expression. The decoration is extended up the towers, and seems in many cases unfinished, for in several of the niches simple blocks of stone are left that have never been carved into completeness. The interior of the porch is supported by one light springing column, whose capital branches into the groined work of a roof all carved with statues and strange arabesques. Within the church the same transition of style is observable. The lacework of the foliage upon the double rank of pillars in the nave is in the late thirteenth-century Gothic, while the capitals in the choir are Byzantine. The whole of the interior is filled with quaint and grotesque carvings, many of which were fortunately untouched by the restorers of

bonne, which anciently formed part of the defences of the archevêché, "bristles with battlements."—Henry James, *A Little Tour in France.*

the seventeenth century. Of the château little more than ruins can be seen, yet it had once a certain notoriety and importance ; it underwent a hot siege from Geoffrey Martel, and it served at various times to shelter Philip Augustus, Charles VII., and Louis XI. It was here, too, that Pierre de Courcelles paraphrased the Song of Solomon in French verses to accompany Clement Marot's new metrical translation of the Psalms.

The road along the river bank turns south to Fontevrault at the village of Montsoreau, which irresistibly reminded us of Bussy d'Amboise and his unfortunate Diana.[1] But the place was long filled with more terrible associations. It served as the rendezvous for a swarm of titled robbers, whose exactions from the voyagers up and down the Vienne and the Loire remained a standing source of annoyance to the district until the days when Richelieu could veil his policy beneath a semblance of benevolence, and relieve the river trade by crushing the feudal rights of Montsoreau. The château must have once been a fine one; the façade is still imposing, pierced with loopholes and supported by strong flanking towers ; its massive walls and masonry attest the goodness of the stone in this district ; the square quarried blocks still line the quays along the

[1] It was in the château of Coutancière at Brain, in the Saumur district, that the scene of Bussy's murder actually took place, as it is described in Dumas's thrilling story.

river here, ready to be floated down to Saumur and the west.

As we slowly mounted the hill the first towers of the Abbey of Fontevrault came in sight, and we were soon parleying for admittance with the sentinel at the great door, for the French Government, with its usual love of strict utility, has turned the old abbey into a vast prison or criminal reformatory, guarded by a regiment. The long lines of silent prisoners in their dull uniforms and round caps file in and out beneath the arches where the white-robed nuns in their black veils used to flit softly to and fro ; one of the many chapels of the abbey is turned into the storehouse for the garrison beer ; lines of great casks fill up the spaces between the pillars that lead from the altar to the door : the strange contrast seemed to strike the keynote of the abbey's history, the history of perhaps the most remarkable institution of its kind in Christendom, and one of the most enduring, for it was as far back as the end of the eleventh century that Fontevrault was founded.

At this time one Robert d'Arbrissel, a monk of "humble but honest parentage" and a scholar of some mark at Paris, had begun to distinguish himself by the fervour and eloquence of his preaching. So great became his renown that Pope Urban II. especially requested him to preach in favour of the Crusades, which just then were moving all the hearts of Europe. The new apostle met with an astonishing

THE ABBEY CHURCH OF FONTEVRAULT, in which are the statues of the Plantagenets, Henry II., Richard I., Eleanor of Guienne, and Isabel of Angoulême.

success. He was soon surrounded by crowds of men and women, good and bad, of every age and degree, who left all to follow him. At the head of this vast multitude, which kept increasing every day, the preacher wandered through town and country until his flock of converts became unmanageable. He had started for the Holy Land ; his charity was compelled to begin nearer home, and at last in this valley he had to stop and make some provision for his strange and ill-assorted company. The contrasts have begun already, these voyagers for Palestine settle by the Loire ; such was the strange beginning of the famous institution that was to shelter the children of kings beneath its roof, and to become famous throughout the length and breadth of Europe.

The queer pilgrimage had ceased by a spring where tradition still remembers the habitation of the robber Evrault, whose stronghold with its conical roof and lantern is still recommended to the wonder of the credulous. The place had a bad reputation, and the owners of the ground found the pious task an easy one of giving up a site to the new colony. Help of more land, of food and clothing, poured in from all sides. The rough clay huts and dividing trenches of the first days of necessity began to give way to more substantial buildings; D'Arbrissel began to draw up rules for his association.

These rules were absolutely different from anything that had been heard of before in such a connection.

At Poitiers or at Lucca there may have been a monastery ruled by an abbess, but never was the principle of the superiority of woman so daringly asserted as at Fontevrault. What was the motive of D'Arbrissel in his plans it is difficult and perhaps profitless to conjecture, but the fact remains that the prosperity of Fontevrault seemed to depend upon its Lady Abbess, and to vary in proportion at once to the strength and the weakness of her authority.

But the founder's motto, "Mère voilà votre fils, fils voilà votre mère," was to have a wider meaning still: the mixed character of his first flock was to be reflected in the future constitution of the community. The first four houses built by the first abbess were for the learned ladies, for penitent women, for lepers, and for monks, and suggested pretty accurately the mingled elements of the first assembly, which had now grown to the respectable figure of 4000. After leaving the strictest rules as to the separation of the sexes, their clothing and their food, and absolutely prohibiting the use of wine ("qui fait même apostasier les sages," say the rules), the good founder died, and was honoured by a funeral at which a great number of his admirers from all parts of the country assisted. The reign of the abbesses had begun; a glance at their names alone, in the list published by M. Malifaud, will give an idea of the importance to which the institution soon attained.

The chief interest of Fontevrault for English

travellers consists in the help and protection always afforded to it by the Plantagenets, whose history was sketched at Chinon ; these English kings, as Counts of Anjou and Touraine, loved the valley of the Loire, and particularly this Fontevrault, where many of their princesses took the veil. Especially was this the case with Henry II., who built the Pont aux Nonnains, which we have already heard of, across the Vienne, near Chinon, to allow, men said, an easy passage from the castle to the abbey and its fair inmates, who were already suspected of something more than ready hospitality.

If the visitor in these days is not so fortunate as to arrive soon after one o'clock on Sunday, he will find the military strictness of the establishment very much against his wanderings in search of knowledge. But he will at least be able to see all that remains intact of the fine church whose buttresses and roofs he has already admired from a distance. The carving round the outer arch upon the western wall that he will pass upon his way towards the entrance of the cloisters is particularly worthy of attention, and the extremely fine circle of pillars round the apse behind the great altar is the best piece of architecture in the abbey.

In a dark little chapel in the right transept of this same mutilated building lie the four Plantagenet statues ; they are those of Henry II., dressed as he was borne out to burial from Chinon, and of his son

Richard Cœur-de-Lion (whose heart is at Rouen). The difference in the expression of father and son is very well rendered ; they lie in the middle of the group. To the left is Eleanor of Guienne, the wife of Henry II., who died here in May 1204 ; she holds a book in her hands. These three figures are of colossal size, hewn out of the tufa rock, and painted. The last, and perhaps the best of the four as a work of art, is of smaller size and carved in wood which has also been coloured : it represents another English Queen, Isabel of Angoulême, one of the most wicked and most beautiful women of her time. She was the daughter of Aymar, Count of Angoulême, and upon the day of her betrothal to Hugues de Lusignan she was carried off by John of England, who put away his first wife Avice to marry this unprincipled and voluptuous beauty ; she bore him the future Henry III. (whose heart was also sent to Fontevrault), and after her English husband's death came back to France to marry her old lover.

These statues, too, have a history of their own. Before 1638 there lay two other figures in the old Cimetière des Rois beneath the cloister of the nuns ; they were the effigies of Jeanne d'Angleterre, the Queen of Sicily, and of her son, Count Raymond of Toulouse, who was represented beating his breast for having embraced the doctrines of the heretics. The sculptor had determined that the count should be penitent after death at any rate, and represent the error of his ways in effigy to after centuries. These last two statues were shattered by the vandals of the Revolution, who broke open all the tombs and scattered their ashes to the winds; they had no leisure to remember that the Plantagenets had built the great dyke beside the Loire and the hospital at Angers, besides numerous other works of public good—Henry II. alone, in time of great famine, supported ten thousand of the poor a day upon his own supplies. The four statues that remained were allowed to moulder into ruins until in 1817 the English Regent asked for them. But the Prefect of the Maine et Loire upheld the right of the province to their possession; the interest and value of the statues had suddenly become apparent. In 1848 Louis Philippe moved them to Versailles; they even travelled through the busy streets of Paris to the Louvre to be repainted, but on their way to England the famous 24th of February intervened, and they were reclaimed finally and irrevocably by the province in which they now rest after these strange wanderings.

"The eastern part of the Abbey of Fontevrault," says Mr. Petit,[1] "though it exhibits slightly pointed arches, has a pure Romanesque rather than a transitional character. The choir is apsidal, with an aisle of the same shape, and radiating semicircular chapels,

[1] *Architectural Studies in France*, new edition, revised by Edward Bell.

which also occur eastward of the transepts . . . the roofs are in general cylindrical." Mr. Petit also saw a "very curious circular structure of the twelfth century," which he considered to be Evrault's hut. But M. Viollet le Duc conclusively proves that it is a fine example of a twelfth-century kitchen, "cuisine qui existe encore mais qui passe pour une *chapelle funéraire*," a third alternative which only shows how little is really understood of mediæval habits.

But after most of the finest of these buildings had been raised, the English wars that harassed France for so many years left their mark upon Fontevrault too in the dismal times of the fourteenth and beginning of the fifteenth centuries. The revenues of the abbey lessened, the community began to grow poor, dissensions arose in its midst, and the more its abbess was slighted the worse the abbey fared. At last the administration fell into vigorous hands; its restoration, which had been begun under great difficulties by Marie de Bretagne, was carried on firmly and successfully by Renée de Bourbon, "Réligieuse, Réformée, Réformante," as she called herself, epithets which show the change in religious opinion which had come over the country.

Meanwhile the abbey was not without illustrious visitors. Francis I. had come with his mother, Louise de Savoie, and the daughter of Louis XII., to confide his natural sister Madeleine d'Orléans to the care of Renée, and we find the loyal abbess later on remembering

TWELFTH-CENTURY KITCHEN AT FONTEVRAULT.

The chimneys are restored from traces still existing in the building, which is now known as the "Tour d'Evrault."—*From Viollet le Duc.*

the visit to good purpose by a substantial contribution to the ransom of the royal princes from their captivity in Spain. In the next reign another visitor appeared with the Duchesse de Guise to be shown to the new abbess, Louise de Bourbon; this was Marie Stuart, who was staying near Saumur, and came to be admired and feasted by the hospitable nuns.[1] The wars of religion later on left their traces too, and the abbey was sharply attacked by some of the royal princes, who had been offended at some plain speaking of the Lady Abbess to King Charles IX. But the gay young King of Navarre, who had apparently helped in this somewhat foolish attempt, was welcomed by the whole community some years afterwards, when on a visit to his aunt with the Princess of Conti. The records of the feast are still preserved: the prince was prudently lodged out of danger beyond the abbey walls.

A visit of Mademoiselle de Montpensier from her dull Court at Blois is worth noticing, for she relates that soon after her arrival screams and loud cries were heard from an inner court; she was told there was a mad woman there, confined in a cell and absolutely naked; she went to see at once, and stayed there until supper. The sight was repeated the next day with a new victim, but the

[1] The monks by this time had learned the gospel of good living from the example of Gargantua. One at least, Gabriel de Puits-Herbaut, had read Rabelais to some purpose, for he published a bitter attack against that author and his works at Paris in 1549.

day after there were no more maniacs to laugh at, so "feeling bored" she left the abbey. The great Richelieu had been seen here before, and seems to have made some efforts to mitigate the extremely severe treatment of the prisoners, evidently without much success.

But the strictness of old D'Arbrissel's rules was relaxing as time went on and abbesses became more worldly. In 1670 Marie Madeleine Gabrielle de Rochechouart[1] is combining the duties of Lady Abbess with a translation of some of Plato's works which was submitted to the scrutiny of Racine. Boileau, Madame de la Fayette, and Madame de Maintenon were among her friends too. Ideas within the abbey were rapidly enlarging. The last abbess, Julie Sophie, daughter of the Duc d'Autin (the name sounds very modern among the cloisters of Fontevrault), arrived in a blaze of splendour so contrary to the directions of the pious Robert that we can see the final ruin of his institution is hard at hand. On the 3d of September 1767 this gay exponent of monastic principles rode into the abbey escorted by fifty carabineers and a jubilant band of hautbois, flutes, and trumpets: in the evening there were fireworks and a big dinner. The abbey had outlived its meaning; the revolutionary edicts swept its inhabitants away, and this last abbess died upon the straw bed of a hospital in Paris.

[1] She was the sister of Madame de Montespan.

We left the abbey echoing with the clank of arms and the trampling of soldiers' feet, hired another horse from the little inn across the street, and drove quickly down the hill towards the Loire. The road to Saumur turns sharply to the left along the river banks between the low line of the hills and the sandy marshes of the stream. Farther along, the slopes are dotted with black windmills, perched on their tiny basements with great arms wide-spread to the breeze; and from every part of this strange cliff curl little wreaths of smoke from hidden chimneys, while a glint of sunlight on a window-pane, that opens suddenly within the rock beneath, reminds the startled traveller that the very ground is teeming with inhabitants.[1] We had noticed this strange sight before among the cliffs of Rochecorbon, but never had it appeared so extraordinary. "It seems," says De Vigny, speaking of the Tourangeaux, "that in their love for so fair a home . . . they have not been willing to lose the least scrap of its soil, the least grain of its sand . . . the very rocks are inhabited, and whole families of labourers from the vineyards breathe the air of these deep caverns, sheltered at night by the same mother earth which they have toiled to cultivate by day." And near Saumur it is the same; for nearly

[1] A traveller along this same road to Saumur tells me it reminded him of the dwellings he had seen in Cappadocia in 1879; he could even "see traces of a columbarium."

eight miles along our way these strange earth dwellings kept surprising us, until we could see upon the slopes above us the terraces and outworks of the Château of Saumur, cut in the thickness of the cliff and strengthened by long lines of low wall.

The old "Murus," as this hill was called, honeycombed with human burrows, served in reality as a kind of last retreat and natural fortress to the old tribes conquered by the Roman invaders, and upon this slope grew the first citadel, the "Truncus," rising like a great oak stem above the conquered country, and spreading out its stony roots across the sandy soil. The fortress that now stands above the town, "foursquare to all the winds of heaven," was probably begun by Geoffrey Martel, son of the Black Falcon, about 1040. It shows signs of having been finished at a much later date.

There is an interesting relic of the Roman invaders preserved in the Museum of the Hôtel de Ville, a perfect specimen of an antique bronze trumpet, curved, and with movable tubes to vary the notes produced. But a memorial of a far older race remains in the great dolmen about a mile and a half to the south of Saumur along the road to Montreuil. This dolmen is the largest in this part of France, and well worth a visit from the student of such antiquities.

Yet another river, the Thouet, joins the Loire close

to Saumur, and the town lies between the two much in the position of Tours between the Loire and Cher. The two towns are alike, too, in the straight line of road that cuts through them in the same direction as the bridge, which at Saumur is a double one, crossing the island and joining both banks of the Loire. It is a fine piece of engineering, and was begun in 1786. This same island has a queer little history of its own, not without interest.

Towards the middle of the fifteenth century,[1] when the good King René of Anjou was reigning, was formed, strangely enough under his patronage, a little republic of fishermen and labourers upon this tiny Venice on the Loire, a Venice whose sole palace was the Château de l'Ile d'Or, the home of the Queen of Sicily. This strange community lived a life apart of hardy toil and independent work, refusing all control save their own rules, and owning no man as their master save the chief whom they elected to watch over the privileges of all and to conciliate their private quarrels. Mock coronations, laughing processions, bright gatherings of men and maidens, gaily went on all the summer in the little island, and even in the days of Louis XVI. an old sailor in the French fleet bore as his proudest title the name of "Roi de la République de l'Ile d'Or." The first "king" was one Faronelle, a royal archer in the guard of Charles VII., who did the

[1] See the *Epoques Saumuroises* of M. B. Coulon.

honours of the island to René's daughter, the Queen of the Loire, who was to leave her beautiful home and become the unquiet Marguerite d'Anjou of the wars of York and Lancaster. Then she was escorted down the river by this "Doge au petit pied," with a flotilla of boats gaily decorated with draperies and flowers, on her way to meet the Duke of Suffolk at Tours, who was to bring her to her English husband.

In front of the gardens of the theatre of Saumur is the Hôtel de Ville, a very perfect example of sixteenth-century architecture with traces of older work. The transition from the times of war to peace is as clearly marked upon its outer face as it is on the double façade of Charles VII. and Louis XII. at Loches. Within, the two ages harmonise more perfectly, and the careful restoration that has been carried out here and there completes what is still one of the finest buildings of the kind in the province. Madame Dacier was born in the Rue du Paradis near here, and the memory of Balzac's Eugénie Grandet came to us as we left the town behind and started on the north bank of the river homewards to Tours.[1]

The railway keeps on this bank past Langeais to Cinq Mars, where it crosses over by a bridge from which the traveller has a fine view of the strange

[1] There was also some severe fighting round Saumur and all through the town during the Vendean War: but space forbids my speaking of it, or indeed of many other points of interest in this town, which well deserves a visit for its own sake.

"Pile de Cinq Mars," which remains an unsolved archæological problem. The towers of Luynes, too, seen from across the water, rise in a cluster high above the plain. It is quite possible that the tall shaft of Cinq Mars forms part of an old system of signalling by beacon fires, of which Langeais would be the last station to the west, and which flamed messages along the valley past Luynes to the Lanterne of Rochecorbon, and as far eastward as Amboise.

# CHAPTER VI

## THREE DUKES OF ORLEANS

"Ingenium velox, audacia perdita, sermo Promptus."—JUVENAL.

THE Italian conversations which Philippe de Commines had begun at the Court of Chinon were already understood and appreciated by a considerable section of his audience; for both as Dauphin and as king, Louis XI. had had far more intimate relations with Italy than was generally supposed. But the connection was one of older standing still, and it is chiefly visible in the story of that House of Orleans which had so many possessions in and about

THE PORCUPINE, BADGE OF LOUIS XII. AND THE HOUSE OF ORLEANS (from the Château of Blois).

Touraine, and from that centre influenced the whole of France. Louis XI. and his immediate successors, Charles VIII. and Louis XII., were far more often in Touraine than at Paris, and the artists of Tours and Poitiers were as familiar with the road to Rome as were those of Paris or of Dijon. Touraine consequently became the centre of the new movement and the home of a strong and flourishing art. By the middle of the sixteenth century the manufacture of tapestry,[1] which had not appeared as a local industry anywhere else in France, had taken such an impetus in Tours that it seemed likely to replace the art of painting. But long before the centre of the artistic movement changed to Paris under Francis I., the school of Tours had won for itself a leading position among the artists of France, and this not only through the example of emigrants from Burgundy like Michel Columbe, for Touraine never owed much to northern influences, but rather through the visits of its own artists to Italy, such as that of Jean Fouquet,[2] the painter of Louis XI., to Rome,

[1] Mrs. Mark Pattison, *Renaissance of Art in France*, vol. i. caps. 1 and 2.

[2] Francesco Florio, a Florentine who lived some time at Tours, mentions Fouquet in 1477, in a description of Touraine written to a friend, as the best painter of that time in France; and Antonio Filarete praises the picture which Jean Fouquet painted on canvas in the Minerva at Rome, representing Pope Eugene IV. with two cardinals, about 1443. From 1470 to 1475 he was paid by Louis XI. for pictures, miniatures, and the design for a tomb, but his chief patron was Etienne Chevalier, treasurer of Charles VII. and Louis, for whom he finished the copy of Boccaccio's "Des Cas des Nobles Hommes et Femmes,"

and through the many Italian artists who came from Rome by Narbonne and passed through Touraine on their way to Paris or to England. Such a traveller, we may suppose, was the unknown artist who built the château of Bury in 1502, for Florimond Robertet. The shower of Italian influences let loose by the expedition of Charles VIII. did not fall upon soil that was unprepared for it. Touraine and all France were already eager to learn more of the Italy with which they had begun to come in contact. An exact idea of this connection with Italy, even though briefly stated, is absolutely necessary for the understanding of what follows in the history of France.[1] John, the good King of France, who died in 1364, had a daughter Isabella, who married Gian Galeazzo Visconti, first Duke of Milan. The palace to which the French princess was brought was filled with priests and friars from the Certosa, with professors from the new college, with poets like Geoffrey

now at Munich, on 24th November 1458, and also a prayer-book in which his taste for Italian architecture is especially remarkable. Nine of the miniatures in the French translation of Josephus in the Bibl. Nat. (Franc. 247) are by Fouquet, and again show the strong Italian influences under which he worked. Examples in England, either of the work of this artist of Tours, or of his school, are the illuminations in the French "Legend de St. Denys" at Christ Church, Oxford, and a prayer-book in the Bodleian Library (Douce, 311). There is also a "Horarium Mariæ Virginis" of 1490 in the same style at Cambridge. See Woermann's *History of Painting*.

[1] See also the genealogical table, especially the houses of Orleans, Valois, Visconti, and Navarre.

Chaucer and Francesco Petrarca, with savants like Philippe de Mézières. England, France, and Cyprus contributed to the brilliant society of the Visconti's Court, where the young heiress, Valentine Visconti, grew up with a keen interest in all the intellectual life before her, and a quick wit to grasp the advantages of her situation: for it soon became evident that this princess, "wise as Medea," would marry into foreign Courts not only as the daughter of Gian Galeazzo, but as the diplomatic agent of the Duke of Milan. She was a "slender woman,[1] rather tall, with a long neck and slim arms, and a bust both full and delicate. The head is small, the hair parted from ear to ear across the middle and looped in pendent braids above the ear. Under this severe coiffure we discern a serious, gentle, placid face, long narrow eyes, a high forehead, a full mouth with pretty pursed lips."

In 1389 she was sent over "bien joyellée et aornée de joyaux" to marry Louis d'Orléans, the handsome brother of Charles VI. of France, bearing with her the Duchy of Asti as her dowry, nearly half a million gold florins, and the promise of the succession to Milan: it was this last portion of the dowry that was to start the quarrel which never ended until Pavia; but even undisputed Asti was a very important foothold for the French in Lombardy. Valentine made a public entry into Paris

[1] Mary Darmesteter, *End of the Middle Ages*, p. 107.

with the Queen.[1] The good citizens were too much afraid of the wisdom of the Visconti serpent to believe it as harmless as a dove, and this mistrust deepened in later years into a definite hatred; but the kind-hearted young King took to Valentine at once, and kept his liking for her to the end.

Her husband Louis, then but eighteen and Duke of Touraine, was already the first knight of chivalry, and among his many passionless amours could find but little time for this new Italian one. Yet one point of contact the newly-married pair possessed—a common love of literature and art, a love which made them still more repugnant to the rude minds of a comparatively unlettered time. With him Valentine could talk over the poems he had made, or the romances of Maître Jean d'Arras; to her he could show, with a full certainty of appreciation, his new

[1] Froissart gives a detailed and animated account of this entry: "Et encore n'avait la jeune dame, qui s'appelait Valentine, entré la cité quand elle y entra premièrement en la compagnie de la reine de France." The people of Paris also presented her with a magnificent litter, as a wedding present, carried by two men dressed in rich Moorish costumes, and containing gold and silver plate to the value of 200 marks. "Le présent réjouit grandement la duchesse de Touraine, et ce fut raison, car il était beau et riche; et remercia grandement et sagement ceux qui présenté l'avaient, et la bonne ville de Paris de qui le profit venait." Juvénal des Ursins also comments on the prodigality of the display made on this occasion. For a picture of a similar entry in the next reign see Bibl. Nat. (fonds Lavallière, 20361), *Chroniques d'Enguerrand de Monstrelet*, where birds are being let loose along the roads as the King beneath a canopy rides past a fountain guarded by two angels.

*Livre de la naissance de toutes choses*, just bought from Jacques Jehan his friend, or discuss the black velvet binding of his new translation of the Bible with its silver clasps enamelled with the arms of Orleans.[1]

But in 1392 the little leisure Louis gave from politics to literature was interrupted by the news of the first outbreak of the King's madness near Mans.[2] "The King was mad," murmured the people, "and the King's brother was a wizard." In the next year his illness was increased by the accident of the

[1] See the catalogue of Charles d'Orléans' books in the Bodleian Library.

[2] Froissart relates what happened.

Early in the hot summer's day, in the forest of Mans, a man dressed in white had suddenly rushed from among the trees to the King's bridle, crying, "Roi, ne chevauche plus en avant, mais retourne ! car tu es trahi." The King was much moved ; "son esprit frémit et son sang se mêla tout." Later on, about midday, as he rode beneath a burning sun that scorched the sandy road and beat upon his black velvet jacket and the scarlet cap upon his head, a careless page let fall a lance upon the helmet of his comrade. The King, fancying, at the clash of steel, that he was attacked by traitors, rushed upon his brother of Orleans with sword drawn, and was with difficulty restrained from killing and wounding all in his path. At last he lost consciousness altogether. "Et lui tournaient à la fois moult merveilleusement les yeux en la tête, ni à nullui il ne parlait." The same author describes the fêtes at the Hôtel Saint Pol in January 1393, when, in a scene which might have suggested to Edgar Allan Poe one of his most ghastly stories, the King and five courtiers (including the Norman who had suggested the unlucky freak) came in dressed as savages in rough flax. The Duke of Orleans imprudently put a torch too near this inflammable material and in an instant there was a quick blaze and shrieks of pain. Fortunately the King was not joined in the circle with the other five but dancing separately, and the Duchesse de Berri saved him by wrapping her cloak round the flames, but his reason never recovered the shock. For a picture of the whole see Bibl. Nat. MSS. Fr., No. 2046.

flaming satyrs at a masked ball, and the people cried out that the old Visconti was a wizard too, and through his daughter cast his spells upon the King of France. But Valentine was far from acting up to such a part. For hours she would patiently sit playing cards with the poor mad King in his dark lonely rooms, and soothe him with the accents of the only voice that he could bear with patience.[1] Even this gentle influence was misconstrued: the people were wild with terror of an unknown danger, "a contagion of fear paralysed the sources of life." Amidst all this horror and uncertainty Valentine left Paris for the Loire.

Meanwhile the Duke of Milan was sending not charms or poisons but ambitious advice to Louis d'Orléans as to an empire to be won in Adria, and a centre of his power at Asti; and when these plans were thwarted by the King of France, Gian Galeazzo tried to enforce his policy by annulling Valentine's claim to the inheritance of Milan, by

[1] He had no knowledge (writes Juvénal des Ursins of the King in 1393) of man or woman, save of the Duchess of Orleans; "car il la voyait et regardait très volontiers, et l'appelait belle sœur. Et comme souvent il y a de mauvaises langues, on disait et publiait aucuns qu'elle l'avait ensorcelé, par le moyen de son père le duc de Milan, qui était Lombard, et qu'en son pays on usait de telles choses."

For a portrait of this historian, who was peculiarly fitted for giving a close account of this reign, see the picture in the Museum at Versailles of "Jean Jouvenel des Ursins" (with a long sword and murderous spurs), "prevôt des marchands de Paris, et Michelle de Vitry sa femme." See also in the Louvre, École Française, No. 652, a fine portrait of Des Ursins, who was Chancellor of France under Charles VII. and Louis XI.

double dealings with the Turk, and other questionable methods of Italian stratagem. As a matter of fact, Louis d'Orléans was feeling too strong to need his help, or indeed that of any man. Before his death he was Duke of Orleans,[1] Lord of Valois and Beaumont, of Asti and Vertus, of Soissons, Blois, and Dreux, with many other dignities, and he used his power unthinkingly for his own ends and unrestrainedly, with all the resources of a man of intellect unfettered by enfeebling scruples.

Already an Augustine Friar, Jacques Legrand, had boldly preached before the Court against licentiousness of manners, and had greatly moved the poor half-witted King. It was no new thing for tyranny and incompetence in rulers to be swiftly punished.[2] All attempts to reconcile Orleans with the house of Burgundy had failed ; he was becoming hated by his own party for the effrontery of his amours, and

[1] The King gave his brother Louis the Duchy of Orleans in 1391, which had reverted to the crown after the death of Philip, Duke of Orleans. This was much objected to at the time by the people of Orleans, as contrary to former promises, but the gift remained a matter of fact.—*Juvénal des Ursins.*

[2] At this time the Queen and the Duke of Orleans were fearfully mismanaging the kingdom during the illness of the King. "Ils étaient devenus un objet de scandale pour la France et la fable des nations étrangères."—*Réligieux de Saint Denis.* At last one was found bold enough to speak out what every one felt and was afraid to utter. "I will speak the truth," said Legrand in his sermon before the Queen, "la déesse Vénus règne seule à votre cour ; l'ivresse et la débauche lui servent de cortège." . . . On the day of Pentecost following he preached before the poor King himself, who sat immediately in front and listened carefully.—*Ibid.*

by the rest for the oppression necessitated by the expenses of his luxury. The down-trodden people prayed, "Jesus Christ in Heaven, send Thou some one to deliver us from Orleans." And a deliverer appeared, if it is just to call a murderer so—John, the impetuous son of the dead Duke of Burgundy. On the 23d of November 1407 Orleans was supping alone with the Queen when a message came that he must go at once to the King. Almost alone, and reckless and gay as ever, he rode through the dark streets of Paris to his brother's house, when he was murdered by the hired assassins of Jean Sans Peur.[1]

The clever and capricious Louis d'Orléans was dead. In him died the most ambitious of a bold and gallant race; a thinker, a savant, an innovator, a friend of poetry and letters, with an extreme facility of eloquence, the very embodiment of unprincipled French strength, which, wedded to the Italian suppleness and finesse of Valentine, was to produce the French Renaissance.[2] Valentine[3] was

[1] As he was passing the Porte Barbette, eighteen men rushed out on him, and at the first blow cut off his hand with an axe. Then by strength of numbers they forced him off his mule and beat his brains out in the road. His page, a young German, tried to protect his master by covering him with his body, but only shared his death.—*Monstrelet.*

See the shorter account given by Saint Gelais.

[2] See the portrait of Louis d'Orléans drawn by the Réligieux de Saint Denis.

It was this "merveilleuse facilité d'élocution" that was faintly reproduced in the elegant versification of his son, Charles the poet.

[3] See the picture of Valentine Visconti in the Museum at Blois.

overwhelmed with grief, and she never recovered from the shock. Her two elder sons were sent to Blois to forget their cares in the garden full of rare flowers and in the library, over *The Battle and Destruction of Troy*, or the mutilated copy, bound in red leather, of the *History of King Arthur and the Holy Grail.*

Of all her children only the bastard Dunois, who "had been stolen from her," had enough courage for the task of vengeance in the future ; that satisfaction in the present was impossible soon became evident. Maître Jean Petit in Paris had accused Louis of "sorcery, high treason against God, and regicide high treason against the King.[1] Charles himself, in letters of pardon to Burgundy, announced that "out of faith and loyalty to us, he has caused to be put out of the world our brother of Orleans." Poor Valentine returned to Blois with Dunois and her children,[2] Charles, the father of Louis XII., John, the grandfather of Francis I., and Philip, Count of Vertus. Here she ceaselessly taught and cared for

[1] Monstrelet gives the extraordinary accusation of Jean Petit at full length. "Il représenta le duc comme un homme souillé de tous les vices," says the Réligieux de Saint Denis, commenting on this same one-sided harangue.

[2] Saint Gelais adds that her daughter married into the house of Brittany, and was the grandmother of Anne de Bretagne, wife of Charles VIII. and Louis XII. of France. "Or peut chacun considérer," he continues, "en quelle désolation demeura cette très noble dame Valentine . . . tous nobles cœurs en devaient avoir grande pitié." She took as the motto of her sadness, "Rien ne m'est plus, plus ne m'est rien."

them, and hoped for vengeance for a year, until her heart broke.

Fortune was not kind to the young Charles in his early days. Apart from the terrible bereavements that had just so suddenly fallen upon him, he had also to deal with a very real distress in money matters, produced by his father's numerous debts, and in 1409 his first wife, Princess Isabelle, died in childbed. No wonder that, amid so many shocks, Charles could not do much. He found himself at the head of the Armagnac party against Burgundy. As a matter of fact he was still merely the standard round which Armagnac (whose daughter Bonne was his second wife) rallied the southern forces. The strange nature of society at this time had produced a series of duels between the great feudal princes, in which a weak and vacillating royalty sometimes sided with one and sometimes with another. In all this Charles could not distinguish yet that his party was the true national party, the party of Joan of Arc and of France. But if his aims were not yet clear to him, his spirit was active and courageous. It is only later[1] that it gave in under captivity, and Charles d'Orléans took "Nonchaloir" for his device, "Insouciance" for consolation, and "Résignation" for his God.

At last, in 1410, preparations began in earnest

[1] See R. L. Stevenson's somewhat depreciatory sketch of Charles d'Orléans in *Men and Books*, p. 236.

for war. Armagnac joined in one great national party the lords of Orleans, Berri, Bourbon, Bretagne, and Alençon. In July Charles is at Amboise, in December at Blois, collecting money, and the next summer his defiance is sent to Burgundy, and deep offence given to the King of France. But there was a rapid change. The momentary political blunder of his alliance with England was remedied by his reconciliation to Burgundy at Blois, and the years 1413 and 1414 are those of Charles's greatest glory. By the Crown are restored all his possessions, and from the University of Paris arrive learned congratulations. That strange "grace de famille" which Charles pre-eminently possessed completely fascinated the poor King, and the Duc d'Orléans, when he was taken prisoner at Agincourt,[1] was one of the most popular young princes in France.

On an October morning in 1415, when the English searched the battlefield after their victory, Charles was found still alive amid a heap of dead

[1] Monstrelet tells us that Orleans was knighted, with several others, just before the battle, after a reconnaissance in force which he had led with the Comte de Richemont. The vanguard, on the day of Agincourt, was led by the Constable, and with him the Dukes of Orleans and Bourbon, the Counts d'Eu and Richemont, and others. Juvénal des Ursins gives an account of the speech in which the King of England in plain terms gives the reasons for their defeat to the French nobles. Those reasons were the misgovernment and ruin already mentioned in connection with Louis d'Orléans. "God," said the English King, "is against you because of your sins." ". . . ils dérobaient tout le peuple et le détruisaient sans raison."

and dying, and by the next month was safely lodged in the Tower of London, where, with rare changes to other places, such as Ampthill and Wingfield, he remained for twenty-five years. Here, where the Duke of Orleans lost his crown, the world gained those poems by which he tried, with memories of the past and graceful fancies of the future, to lighten the captivity that changed him into the heavy old man of his later life.

In politics his place is a curious one: he was a remnant of the front rank that fell at Agincourt, and by its fall made easier the levelling policy of Louis XI. He was the "Sleeping Beauty of Feudalism,"[1] who fell asleep when the great lords were feudal gods, and awoke in a France that had begun to realise the power of royalty. His position as a poet is as strange. His verses are still charming, for he was a poet of no school, and, like so many unknown ballad-writers of the time, sang naturally and easily as the lark beneath the open sky. They were written at the very beginning of the poetic fervour brought on by the Renaissance, and at the very birth of the new art of printing; but they were as little known in his own day as they were recognised by later times, and this because their pure "finesse" was out of place in a century to which Villon only appealed by his intellectual

[1] M. Charles d'Héricault, Preface to *Poésies Complètes de Charles d'Orléans.* Jannet Picard, 1874.

vigour and his popular grossness. In an age when ease, simplicity, and grace were sacrificed to imitations of the classics, his poems were equally disdained by the exclusive and pedantic school, to whom Charles d'Orléans was as "profanum vulgus." The imprisonment that gave their originality to Charles's verses freed them also from the fetters of an Alain Chartier or a Meschinot.[1] The delicacy of his touch may be seen in the lines of the fourteenth Rondeau in Héricault's edition—

"Les en voulez-vous garder
Ces rivières de courir,"

or in the numerous sonnets to Springtime, such as—

"Le temps a laissie son manteau
De vent, de froidure et de pluye;"

or in the sad lines to Old Age (Rondeau ccxci.)—

"A! que vous m'ennuyez, Vieillesse."

Many of these were written in the last years of his life, many (some of them in English, too) in the long days of his captivity, in which he lingered on amid vain hopes of release. Henry V. died giving no word of hope. D'Alençon and D'Eu had left their prisons, but Charles d'Orléans refused to recognise the English King as suzerain. It was Jeanne d'Arc who really made the first step towards his

[1] Meschinot, for instance, wrote "poems which can be read in thirty different ways, any word being as good to begin with as any other."—*Saintsbury.*

deliverance, Jeanne who must have thought of him while she took English prisoners for exchange, and who delivered his Orleans, which was besieged contrary to all promises made him by the English King. But his estate languished without him. Dunois had been captured, and the messenger who brought ill news said nothing of the good work that his friends were doing. Already, in 1427, hearing in the Tower of London of the English advance along the Loire, Charles had feared for his books at Blois, and sent them by the Seigneur de Mortemart to his house in Saumur. They were moved farther on to La Rochelle, until eight years later, the danger having passed, Charles writes to have them sent back to Blois, and directs especial search to be made at Orleans for a cherished little volume stamped with the arms of Berry.

In 1433 he uselessly gave in his submission to the King of England, who, as the grandson of Charles VI., was posing as the real heir of France. But seven more years dragged on before the Duke of Burgundy, the son of Jean Sans Peur, arranged his deliverance. It was granted now, for the policy of England was at this time to weaken the royal power by encouraging the great barons, as it had been before to weaken feudality by keeping Orleans prisoner. At last his cry was answered.

"Qui m'ostera de ce tourment
Il m'achetera plainement,

A tousjoursmès à heritage
Tout sien seray, sans changement,
Mettroye corps et ame en gage."

His marriage with Marie de Clèves (his second wife was dead long ago) produced enough money by her dowry to bring his ransom within the bounds of possibility. The friendship of Charles d'Orléans with the son of his father's murderer is an interesting and touching trait in this strange story of his release. His dreamy, romantic nature was not made for the sterner necessities of revenge.[1]

In 1440 he returned to France with all the ideas of 1415, and took up his abode at Blois, where his "good fat face," his strong Italian nose and chin, are seen among physicians and astronomers, watching over his choir, listening to the harpers, and reading the ballads that everybody wrote to please him: no one paid the least attention to Charles's own verses, the only ones that were to live. During the first few years of freedom, the time there was left to him from the business of collecting his ransom, to which every one contributed, he spent in happily wandering about and "seeing France"[2] after his long absence,

[1] "Or voyez que c'est des jugements de Dieu. Car les pères de ces deux seigneurs avaient été les plus grands ennemis qui oncques furent." —*Saint Gelais*.

[2] "Et là (Blois) et ailleurs partout où il passa, le peuple en était aussi réjoui que si c'eût été un ange qui fut descendu du ciel," says Saint Gelais. The same author tells us that at this time Charles d'Orléans instituted an order or livery, called "Le Camail," on which hung a

just as some years after he travels abroad and dreamily inspects his property at Asti. He took his pleasures gently ; old age was coming on him all the quicker for his long captivity ; and he lived quietly in his home at Blois.

> "Pource qu'on jouxte à la quintaine
> A Orléans je tire à Blois,
> Je me sens foulé du harnois
> Et veulx reprendre mon alaine."

In 1444 he had the pleasure of leading his own old gaoler, the Duke of Suffolk, from Blois to Tours, where the peace was made that followed the marriage of Marguerite d'Anjou, and Charles seems to have celebrated the occasion with much light-heartedness.

> "Durant les trèves d'Angleterre
> Qui ont esté faittes à Tours,
> Par bon conseil, avec Amours
> J'ai prins abstinence de guerre."

But he found himself compelled at last to go abroad. In 1422, John and Charles d'Orléans being both in prison and Henry VI. of England crowned King of France, Asti had sent for protection to Filippo Maria Visconti, Duke of Milan. Three years before Charles's deliverance Francesco Sforza was in possession at Asti as lieutenant ; but shortly

hedgehog, which was given as an honourable badge to several of the notable French knights.

His son, Louis XII., used the porcupine as his badge, which is still carved on the walls of the Château of Blois.

afterwards Dunois went out to carry on negotiations and open up the quarrel afresh. The old Duke of Milan wearily got rid of him ; but another factor appeared in the Dauphin Louis, whose alliance with Milan soon became clear, and Dunois, enraged, insisted on Asti being immediately given up ; this was done, for Francesco Sforza was playing for the higher stake of Milan, after the duke's death, against the unexpected heir, Alfonso of Arragon, King of Naples. Then Charles d'Orléans himself came out to Asti, but only to make promises to Venice, to lay great stress on the real friendship between himself and Burgundy, and to do nothing more practical than rhyming verses with Antonio Artesano. The hesitation of Charles gave Francesco Sforza his opportunity ; he rode into starving Milan with his soldiers' armour hidden by the welcome loaves of bread, and took the city. This was as unwelcome to the Dauphin as its occupation by Charles d'Orléans would have been, but a sudden rise of independent spirit repulsed for a time the French claims on Milan and on Genoa too.

Charles had gone home again with much new learning in Italian rhymes and fashions, many new ideas on dress and arms and architecture, which were to be worked out as opportunity should serve at his own Court. There was great economy in this quiet little household at Blois, but it was soon lighted up by the presence of young Pierre de Bourbon, who was adopted into the family. In 1457 a daughter,

Marie, was most unexpectedly born to the house of Orleans, and among the first congratulations were the verses of the poet Villon, who, until 1465, held a small position in the Court at Blois. He sings of the young princess[1] with various tags of Latin such as Charles himself loved to put into his rhymes, feeling a little constrained at the sudden change from his usual vigorous language to the phrases of a courtly salutation. But a still greater astonishment was to come.

In 1462 Charles was receiving the amused and delighted congratulations of the whole of France at the birth of the young son who was to become Louis XII. This event was not only startling but positively distasteful to Louis XI., who had quite looked forward to quietly absorbing[2] the possessions of the heirless Duke of Orleans into the Crown domain, and indeed came to Blois that very year to try and get Asti from him. But he failed, and the elegant and picturesque life at the château went on gravely and quietly as ever, amid a twittering of ballads and the sound of minstrels' singing, while Villon, René d'Anjou, Robertet, Jacques de la Trémouille, or Boulainvilliers came and played chess[3] with the old duke, or wrote

[1] Of Charles's two daughters, one married the Comte de Foix, the other was an Abbess of Fontevrault.

[2] Compare the policy of the same King later on in marrying this very child Louis to Jeanne de France, with the expressed desire of bringing the line of Orleans to an end.

[3] From a miniature in a fifteenth-century MS., "Les Trois Ages de l'Homme," supposed to be by Estienne Porchier, we can imagine what a

him playful roundels, until at seventy-four years of age Charles died, "in all the practices of Christian charity," at Amboise.[1]

The young Louis d'Orléans had been told by his mother of the claims of Valentine Visconti ; but the influence of the house of Orleans in Italy, especially after Dunois' death, was very weak, and for some time young Louis himself felt the pressure of the King's policy of consistently weakening the noble houses, until he was forced into marrying the deformed Jeanne de France much against his will.[2] But at twenty we hear of him as the best archer, horseman, and man-at-arms at Court, and when, some ten years later, the pressure on him was relieved by the death of Louis XI., he at once began to flourish and grow strong in spite of the opposition of Anne de Beaujeu, Regent for the young Charles VIII. But Anne was too capable to be lightly put aside. With all her father's vigour and astuteness, she favoured the cause of civil war in England, she encouraged revolt in Flanders, and having shaken off possible foreign foes, she hurled the royal army commanded by La Trémouille against the Breton,

game of chess looked like at this time. Four men are standing round the board and watching, one player with his piece lifted waits while he thinks over his move. This player has been thought to be Louis XI. in one of the rooms at Plessis-lez-Tours.

[1] See the portrait of Charles d'Orléans by Rulmann, after a miniature on vellum in the Bibliothèque Royale.

[2] She was "sterile, brutta e quasi uno mostro," says Guicciardini, *Storia Fiorentina* (*opere inedite*, vol. iii.), p. 183.

German, and English forces of the Duke of Orleans, conquered him at Saint Aubin du Cormier,[1] and threw him into prison. But Louis had not allowed schemes of revolt to take up all his days in Brittany: he found time to make love to the ambitious little heiress, Anne de Bretagne, who had been by no means satisfied with her marriage by proxy to the Emperor Maximilian.[2] This was not unknown to Anne de Beaujeu, and Louis d'Orléans was offered his freedom if he could arrange a marriage between Charles VIII. and Anne. He accomplished this somewhat delicate mission successfully, and returned home, to the warlike Court of Charles VIII., where the cautious Maréchal de Gié was vainly striving to suppress the military aspirations of the King.

These dreams of conquest were further encouraged by the embassy of Venice asking for help against Naples, Milan, and Ferrara. The policy of Louis XI. began to bear fruit. Louis d'Orléans himself had already been offered Milan in the place of Ludovico il Moro, who had seized the Regency, but this offer at first came to nothing amid the constant changes of Italian intrigue. At last, in 1494, Ludovico was hailed Duke of Milan, and called in the French to help him, adroitly reminding Charles of the old

[1] See *Mémoires de la Trémouille*, xiv. 140.

[2] "L'envoyé imperial (un maigre seigneur allemand) plaça, selon l'usage, sa jambe nue dans le lit de la jeune Duchesse. Mais Madame Anne ne fut pas contente."—*Coignet.*

claim to Naples.[1] In this extraordinary Italian expedition Orleans met Charles at Asti, and was obliged to stay there ill near Il Moro, who was trying to guide this tempestuous invasion that seemed likely to have far more success than he had bargained for. Knowing that his claims would not be allowed, but encouraged by secret offers of help from Venice, Orleans soon began to claim Milan for himself; but Ludovico Sforza's subtle policy necessitated not only the revoking of the imperial letters with which Il Moro had provided himself, but quite new letters establishing the Visconti claim. Sforza's title had been gravely recognised, too, in Venice before the imperial ambassadors. Nothing remained but an appeal to arms. So, quite contrary to orders, Orleans sent twenty knights forward suddenly to occupy Novara, and before the month was out had seized the town. His next step should have been an immediate attack on Milan, but he foolishly waited till Milan was protected and Novara closely surrounded by the enemy. Three fearful months of siege followed, in which the duke endeared himself to his soldiers by his brave endurance of the same

[1] It is impossible to give in one short chapter all the tortuous changes of Italian politics at this time. The actual state of affairs at the beginning of 1494 was, that Ludovico was Regent of the infant heir to the Duchy of Milan, his nephew. Wishing to strengthen his position, he called in the French, and crushed what weak claims could be opposed to his assuming the actual title of duke by obtaining an imperial letter in his own favour. See Commines (vii. 6), who had his information from the Venetian ambassador.

privations as themselves. At last he was released by composition, and to his disgust his claim was left unsupported by the King.[1]

A year after Charles would have sent him out again, but Louis saw the prospect of a higher stake at home, for the Dauphin had just died. Ambassadors to Amboise from Florence, asking for help against Milan, could no better persuade him, for now the King himself was ill. On the 8th of April 1498 he heard the soldiers round his courtyard at Blois crying, "Vive Louis XII. !"

The Italian claims were forgotten for the moment, but were soon to be revived. The snake of Italy seemed to have a terrible fascination for the

[1] Commines tells the whole story of this impolitic business of Novara. The Duke of Orleans, when Louis XII., often showed signs of an incapacity for foreign politics and strategy, which he only redeemed by the excellence of his government at home. The taking of Novara was against orders. "Et avoit esté escrit," says Commines, "à mon seigneur d'Orléans, et aux capitaines, qu'ils n'entreprissent riens contre le duc de Milan, mais seulement entendissent à garder Ast."—VIII. iii.

After the town was taken no proper provision for a siege was made, no consideration given to the unsafe position of the place itself: "car elle est à dix lieues de Milan et estoit force que l'un (Duke of Milan or Orleans) eut tout."—VIII. ix. The sufferings of the garrison from hunger were terrible: "on n'avoit vu de longtemps si grosses nécessités ; et cent ans avant que fussions nés, ne souffrirent gens si grande faim comme ils souffrirent léans."—VIII. ix. . . . "il mourut bien deux milles hommes, que de faim que de maladie."

Nor could Orleans fairly complain, after the treaty that had been made with some difficulty for his release, that the King was in no hurry to do more for a subordinate whose rash action had seriously inconvenienced him at the moment, and was to lead to yet more trouble in the future. On the mistakes of Louis XII. in Italy see Machiavelli, *Prince*, cap. iii.

hard-headed Frenchmen, who all the time half dreaded the nation whose influences they were so fast absorbing—and these influences grew year by year, from the first touch of the pure early Renaissance brought by Louis d'Orléans, until the days when Francis I., with Italian blood in his veins from both sides of his house, flooded France with the influences of the later spirit that was but a decaying remnant of the old fresh impulses, that brought a Catherine de Medicis instead of a Valentine Visconti.

## CHAPTER VII

### LOCHES

"Tant d'allées et tant de venues,
Tant d'entreprises incongnues,
Appoinctemens rompus, cassez,
Traysons secrettes et congnues,
Mourir de fièvres continues,
Bruvaiges et boucons brassez,
Blanez scellez en secret passez!"

GRINGOIRE,
*Le Jeu du Prince des sots et mère sotte.*

THE river Indre crosses the south-east frontier of Touraine near Châtillon, and flows between Loches and Beaulieu till it reaches Corméry, where it turns sharply to the west, and passing the keep of Montbazon, winds slowly round the turrets of Azay-le-Rideau towards its meeting with the Loire below Langeais. Perhaps no greater contrast between two such buildings exists as between the two guardians of the Indre, the sculptured bridges of Azay-le-Rideau and the massive walls of Loches. Placed in a most important strategical position between the valleys of the Cher and the Vienne, Loches is itself guarded by Montbazon and Montrichard, and forms the lowest

PORCH OF THE *Église Collégiale* AT LOCHES.

**In the foreground is an old Roman Altar, now used for Holy Water.**

point of the line of fortresses that protect the southern approaches of the Loire.

One of the chief features in the flat landscape through which the railway from Tours passes is this keep of Montbazon, a vast square mass of masonry rising suddenly from the ground, the donjon of the ruined castle of Foulques Nerra. Poised upon one corner stands a colossal statue of the Virgin, evidently of recent erection, with much better effect than at first sounds possible; distance perhaps lent something of majesty, as it stood high above the fields and trees looking down upon the sunlit plain. The country past Reignac and Chambourg stretches in an endless flat expanse of land cultivated over every inch with that care of which French peasants seem alone to have the secret, and watered by the "ribbon of the Indre."

Above this plain rises the hill crowned with the towers of Loches,[1] like Mont St. Michel above the sands of the north coast. The houses, thrown together along steep and twisted streets, cluster beneath the walls that guard the castle, and the eye rises from the Tour de St. Antoine in the little "place" beneath, towards the donjon keep and the pinnacles of the Collegiate Church. A sharp ascent from this first tower, which is of sixteenth-century work, and used to contain the

[1] The name seems to be derived from the word *loc* or *luc*, the same as loch = lake. Possibly the Indre used to overflow in earlier days.

bells of the town, leads upward past the tiny Hôtel de Ville to the first line of walls. There is a plan drawn in 1699 showing the first extent and strength of these fortifications, which circled the whole area of the scattered buildings of the castle, and isolated it like an island from the surrounding country.

STEEPLE OF THE *Église Collégiale* AT LOCHES.
*From Viollet le Duc.*

The buildings have three distinct divisions: the Collegiate Church in the midst, with the donjon and the prisons to the east, and on the other side the actual château, which is in part still inhabited, looking down upon the western plain. And if the dungeons will leave the most lasting impression on the traveller, it is this church which is the great architectural feature of the place. "In France," says Viollet le Duc, "exactly on the border line which separates buildings with cupolas from those with none, there is a strange and unique monument in which the influences of Oriental art are blended with the methods of construction adopted in the north at the beginning of the twelfth century. This is the Collegiate Church of Loches: a monument unique in the world, perfect in its kind, and of a savage beauty." It was round the first building raised on this spot that the castle and town of Loches began: here, in 450, St. Eustache built a church, which was dedicated by Childebert to La Madeleine. On the ruins of this early structure was built the Église Collégiale by Geoffrey Greygown in 962, and consecrated by Hardouin, Bishop of Tours, under the patronage of King Clothaire. In 1180 began the church as it now stands, all broken into points and angles, with not so much as the line of the roof horizontal.[1] I will not trust myself to attempt the architectural description of this extraordinary building. "It consists," says Mr. Petit,[2] "of two steeples of nearly the same height though different detail, flanked one of them by an apsidal projection, the other by a low rectangular porch, while the

[1] There is hardly any wood in the construction at all—white stone is used throughout.

[2] *Architectural Studies in France*, new edition, revised by Edward Bell.

intermediate space is occupied by two large octagonal pyramids of stone, nearly in contact with each other as well as with the belfry towers. How are these pyramids supported? What we have taken for the front is the side; the flanking towers are in reality a central and western tower; the two pyramids of stone form the roof of the nave, and not only externally but internally also"—hollow pyramids whose tops are lost in shadow, and give an indefinable feeling of terror. The gray weather-beaten stones upon its outer walls give a striking contrast to the cool white masonry within, very much like the effect of a glimpse of the interior of the cathedral at Christ Church from the Quad, without the richness of detail and carving in the later work, and with an added beauty all its own.

Through a very fine Romanesque porch, whose grotesque carvings seem designed to enforce the saying, "laid comme le péché mortel," and in which is a strange old cylindrical vessel, now used for holy water, we passed into this cold and quiet building, where some lines of the old tinted decorations were still left upon the stones, and the rich light from the windows above the altar at the farther end fell softly on the arches of the choir. The construction of the masonry is particularly noteworthy, and especially the corbelling of the roof of the nave, which is divided into two square compartments by a pointed arch of one square order.

INTERIOR OF THE *Église Collégiale* AT LOCHES,
showing the hollow pyramids which form the roof of the nave.—*From Viollet le Duc.*

The aisles are quite independent of the main building. The pictures and trifles added by a later day had done less to spoil this church than in almost any other building of the same size we had seen. There was, it is true, one small chapel filled with such incongruities, but it was out of sight ; and the whole effect was pleasing in the extreme—the peculiarity of the building, its two white funnel-like domes opening upward to the roof, giving it an originality and charm which nothing could quite efface.[1]

A smiling verger, who refused to take our timorous denials, candle in hand led us down some steps to the right of the choir, and showed with quiet pride a subterranean chapel connected by a passage, long since blocked, with the castle. This is the crypt, situated under the south apse, which is small, but seems original. Here Louis XI., so it is said, came to pray, below ground and secret even in his devotions, in this castle so full of subterranean mysteries. Some strange paintings of saints and their accessories have also been discovered here beneath the plaster. The most beautiful ornament of the church in earlier times was the tomb of Agnes Sorel, which has been moved to the Tour d'Agnès, whither we next turned.

[1] Mr. Petit says that this church is later than the earliest specimens of the Perigueux dome and earlier than the Angevin vaultings, and therefore may be a link between the two ; the leaving of the roofing open makes this an exceptional and distinct case.

There is a door straight on past the church which is opened by a smiling old woman and discloses the Castle of Loches. We had come prepared for horrors, forgetting that the older portion of the château, that lay behind us to the east, was the place of the dungeons ; and we were surprised. Everything wore an astonishingly humane aspect. This was partly accounted for by the fact that the Sous-Préfet of the district lives here, which gives the place a strange feeling of life and habitation ; and we fortunately did not see M. le Sous-Préfet to dispel the illusion of antiquity by his modernised appearance—in anything but chain mail and wearing a formidable sword, he would have been disappointing.

Further impressions became still more peaceful. We were first led to the little quiet chapel, lighted by two windows of stained glass, where repose the remains of Agnes Sorel, " une douce et simple colombe plus blanche que les cygnes, plus vermeille que la flamme," as the inscription tells us. She lies draped in a dress whose folds have a singular charm of outline, with her feet resting upon two lambs that innocently suggest her name. The face is beautiful still, even in the marble restored with plaster as it is now, and I could believe that truly in life " son visage avait l'éclat des fleurs en printemps." Peace to her ashes—after so many violating hands have touched them. Even the revolutionists could not completely desecrate the tomb they tried to rifle. Whatever else she may have been, we may remember that "Demoiselle de Seurelle, Dame de Beauté," placed her influence with Charles VII. on the side of good and, when need was, on the side of patriotism. The verses of Francis I. have a truer ring than the prudery of later days—

> "Gentille Agnès, plus d'honneur tu mérites
> (La cause étant de France recouvrir)
> Que ce que peut dedans un cloître ouvrir
> Close nonnain ou bien dévot hermite."

Marie d'Anjou, the gentle and kind Queen of Charles VII., always recognised the good qualities of Agnes; and even the Dauphin, whose spiteful malice against her frequently broke out, when he was King refused to let her tomb be moved from the church, "unless her bequests were taken from it too." So for a time her body stayed there. Her executor in the many pious bequests of her will was the famous Jacques Cœur, who had not yet fallen into unmerited disgrace. One tangible witness of the results she had no slight hand in bringing about is the "cul de lampe" on the tower at the west angle of the palace —a carved soldier, on the point of being beaten, thrusting through, in his last effort, the English leopard. "Douce dans ses discours, apaisant les querelles," Agnes made far better use of her opportunities than many others, who have only succeeded in adding to a position equivocal at best a reputation decidedly unfortunate.[1]

The tower in which lies the tomb of Agnes Sorel was the tower in which she often lived, and, as might have been expected, it communicates with the apartments of the King. These present a fine façade of simple and strong architecture, faced by a terrace excellently restored, and looking down from a height that already seems astonishing upon the houses beneath, which have grown for ages round the immediate precincts of the castle, and within the shelter of its widespreading walls. The restoration of this part of the building was done with equal thoroughness and good taste.

Joined to the apartments of Charles VII. comes the façade of Louis XII., with a contrast just sufficient to denote the change of time from war to peace, from buttresses and meurtrières to carved wide windows, and not too striking to produce any discordant effect upon the building as a whole. It was in these buildings that Louis XII., after the death of Anne de Bretagne, lived so unwisely and so well with the young and beautiful sister of the English King, whom he married in 1514. Being "fort antique et débile," as Louise de Savoie says bitterly in her Journal, he could not stand the strain of a complete change in his habits of life, and died soon

[1] See the account of Agnes Sorel's visit to Paris in 1448, in the *Journal d'un Bourgeois de Paris.*

THE CHÂTEAU OF LOCHES FROM BENEATH.

On the left the tower of Agnes Sorel, next to the façade of Charles VII., on the right the château of Louis XII.

afterwards. Here, too, in 1547, came his successor Francis on one of those feverish hunting excursions which immediately preceded his death.

We had but too short a time to pace the terrace and look down upon the view before the summons of our old lady and the impatient jingle of her keys called us away. Under the famous chestnut tree of Francis I., a tree that looks healthy enough to live as many years more as it has done already, and to grow still larger and more beautiful, we passed behind the main buildings to a little turret staircase, from which we were able to remark the beautiful details of the carving on the upper part of the house from the vantage-ground of a high window; I noticed the sitting hound which was one of the badges of Louis XII., and a strikingly powerful carving of a jester's head within its curling hood projecting from the line of stone beneath the roof. This same roof, too, presented a magnificent mass of oak beams and solid carpentry as we looked up at them from the floor of the top story which had once been the Salle des Gardes, so we were informed, though why they were so far removed from practicable ground we could not at the time conjecture.

The staircase leads to the oratory of Anne de Bretagne, a tiny little chamber completely covered with carvings in the stone and plaster—the chief device was the ermine and the twisted cord repeated in endless variations, which were strangely picturesque at last.[1] Some traces of colour still cling to the walls, and a most delicate piece of stone carving hung from the keystone of the arch above us, like the tracery of lace upon a lady's handkerchief. We had entered through a door made in what was originally the altar of the little chapel, with a beautiful stone canopy above it, and went out through the old entrance into an apartment behind, which had apparently been used as a prison during the Revolution. Several of its inmates had left inscriptions, poetical and otherwise, upon the

THE ORATORY OF ANNE DE BRETAGNE AT LOCHES.
Decoration showing her emblems of the ermine and the twisted cord.

[1] The meaning of this symbol is much debated. The knotted cord untied again can hardly refer to the very brief space of Anne's widowhood having been spent here, nor is it a symbol peculiar to herself. She is said to have recommended it to many of the ladies about her Court, and possibly took it from her father, whose house was peculiarly devoted to St. Francis of Assisi.

walls; one of these ended with the word "Esperance" in larger writing than the rest: a prisoner might, at all events, have more hope within these walls, swept by the winds of upper air, than in the ghastly dens below ground that we were soon to see.

In a corner of this same room were thrown two dusty and torn portraits of royal personages—"Presented by the Emperor" was written on their frames. They were but one more sign of the tempest of Republican sentiment which had left several marks on Loches from the first outburst of 1790 to the Republic of to-day. If there is one thing that Loches is not, it is not democratic; and we much admired the finesse with which the Republican official was ensconced in the most habitable portion of the castle, while the more dreary and appalling ruins were left to inspire a becoming horror of even the relics of criminal and despotic monarchy.

We had left the oldest part of Loches to the last. M. Mabille thinks that perhaps the earliest château was one of the rare ones built by the Merovingians in the sixth century, but though such an one may have existed, no older building than the gigantic donjon keep of Foulques Nerra is now to be seen in this part of the castle. It is like that of Rochester, but the flat pilaster buttresses often seen in Norman work [1] have in this example massive shafts engaged one in each, forming a semi-cylinder. The stone for

[1] Petit, *op. cit.*

the building was taken from the great trench still to be seen between the castle and the hill of Vignemont. The Black Falcon, who had built Montbazon and Montrichard to protect this, the most important fortress, from attacks from Blois and Chaumont, could also overawe the neighbouring settlement at Beaulieu, where he built the abbey,[1] and whose inhabitants were frequently quarrelling with the men of Loches concerning certain market privileges and other questions, which seem to be equally unsettled at the present day. We looked up from beneath at the four great walls or rather cliffs of stone which formed the keep, where traces of four stories still were visible, reached by stairs cut in the thickness of the wall, and capable of containing 1200 men. The question of "supplies" was settled by a dark and extremely unwholesome-looking hole sinking into the bowels of the earth, through which the food for the garrison was raised. The whole had evidently been built more with a view to durability and strength of resistance than elegance or grace ; a relic of the older days which was almost deserted by the time Francis I. had metamorphosed the feudal castles of Touraine into so many royal hunting-seats.

But the strength of Loches had its advantages

[1] According to the hideous fashion of desecrating tombs to sift the ashes of their dead for relics, and provide mouldering problems for archæological disputes, the coffin of Foulques Nerra has been broken open to see that he was really buried in Beaulieu. Even Agnes Sorel could not rest undisturbed by the unholy curiosity of "explorers."

in its own time. It was as useful to the English Plantagenets as it had been to their Angevin forefathers. The first siege that Cœur-de-Lion undertook on his return from imprisonment was this of Loches, held by Guy de Laval for the French King. Philip lost it for a time, but took it from John Lackland, who was not strong enough to protect the forces of the widowed Berengaria. Passing for a while from the Crown as a reward to the Constable of France, Loches was reclaimed as a royal residence by St. Louis in a special letter from "Egypt on the banks of the Nile." John the Good came here on his way to defeat and captivity at Poitiers, and the next French King who dwelt at Loches was only "Roi de Bourges." Charles VII. and his Queen Marie d'Anjou possessed but the shadow of a kingdom before Agnes Sorel ended the work that Jeanne d'Arc had begun.

But the presiding spirit of the memories of Loches is Louis XI. Already as Dauphin he had troubled the place with the intrigues of the Praguerie. Here the Bastard of Bourbon, Antoine de Chabannes,[1] and other captains "avec foison de gens d'armes," came to meet him and arrange for the conspiracy at Moulins. He had been at Loches under governors since about 1438, and chafed there after having tasted the sweets of command in Poitou and Dauphiné, where he had been sent to chase out

[1] Monstrelet, *Chroniques*, liv. ii. cap. ccxlv.

the "écorcheurs." [1] The flatteries of his servants, and the suggestions of universal discontent made by his courtiers, gave fuel to the fire of ambition that burnt within him. The King crushed the conspiracy and tried to give the restless Dauphin occupation in conquering the rebellious Count of Armagnac and in some very savage fighting against the Swiss. Louis' wife, Margaret of Scotland, who had sailed to her wedding at Tours pursued by English ships, died at twenty-two about this time, and certain dark suspicions clung to the Dauphin's reputation from which he never shook himself free all his life. His other characteristics soon began to show themselves too. In constant and open opposition to his father, he was at one time obliged to fly to Burgundy, and actually writes in excuse, "pour ce que, comme vous sçavez, mon bel oncle de Bourgogne a intention de brief aller sur le Turc, à la défense de la foi catholique."

It was while he was listening to the *Cent Nouvelles Nouvelles* at his distant Court at Genep, that he heard tidings of his father's death, and at last seized the power he had been thirsting for so long. His first business was to revenge himself upon his father's friends, his next to raise extraordinary sums in pitiless taxation. One mistaken

[1] For the terrible state of France in 1439, during the murders and depredations of these écorcheurs, see Olivier de la Marche, *Chroniques*, I. ccxliii. "Tout le tournoiement du royaume de France était plein de places et de forteresses, vivant de rapines et de proie."

bargain at this time proved an exception to his usual rule of cunning and intrigue. After he had moved from Amboise to Tours he was there cajoled by the Pope into abolishing the Pragmatic Sanction, and seems to have got nothing in return but a holy sword.

But in spite of the dark shadow which this monarch had managed to cast over all Touraine during the process of encouraging its wealth and commerce, we cannot fail to be impressed with the strong sense of a vigorous personality; of a man who, with all his faults, resolved to rule, who if he could not be loved determined to be feared. Scott's masterly presentment of Louis XI. in *Quentin Durward* will be in the mind of all travellers in Touraine, and Chateaubriand has thrown into strong relief the strange contrasts visible in this unique character, who was as immoral in his private life as he was tyrannically severe in public judgments.[1]

This Louis, who made his servants heralds, and his barbers Ministers of State, whose only confidants, says Voltaire, were low-born men with hearts lower than their stations, who regained by unscrupulous cunning what he lost by the natural depravity of his

[1] It is a curious fact for students of heredity that the daughter of Marguerite de Sassenaye, the mistress of Louis, married Aymar de Poitiers, an ancestor of the fair Diana whom we shall meet at Chenonceaux. It is strange, too, that this same Diana's husband was Louis de Brézé, Grand Seneschal of Normandy, whose father had married the daughter of Charles VII. and Agnes Sorel.

character, who showed conspicuous address and bravery when a youth of twenty, died at last a cowardly old man amidst despicable scenes of senile debauchery and terror. He died after having made justice secure and strengthened France by politics and war; and yet before his death he had killed by fair means or foul more than four thousand of his subjects, and, as in the case of the family of Nemours, shown the last degree of cold and calculating cruelty—a cruelty which left but few great men worth the name in France, and ground down the nation to the tranquillity of a gang of galley slaves: in all this his only limitation was betrayed in his manners, his head never wavered, for (until his death) he was at any rate no coward. "I can easily dare," says Commines, "to give this praise to Louis—never have I seen a man bear up so stoutly in adversity."[1] But the contrasts go still farther. The King who chained up the volumes of the Nominalists protected the first printers from Germany, and the freedom of the printing press received its first real encouragement in France from the most tyrannical monarch on the French throne.

One distinct aim can be seen throughout the changing actions of Louis' reign: his object was not so much to extend the outward boundaries of his

[1] For a longer description of Louis' character see Commines, I. x., in which the significant words occur, "il était naturellement ami des gens de moyen état, et ennemi de tous grands qui se pouvaient passer de lui."

kingdom, but still more to crush feudality within, and to create absolute monarchy. "The Genoese have given themselves up to me," he writes, "and I hand them over to the devil." That Louis' foreign policy was not really so restricted in its aims as used commonly to be thought, is becoming more and more clear, but it is by the principle of centralisation that all his actions, good or bad, were dominated, and for this necessary task he was the necessary man.

In his enlightenment and his superstition, his cruelty and his great plans for France, Louis is a true type of his age, which was that of transition from dying mediævalism to the new life which the art of the Renaissance was bringing. It had been long in coming to France. One hundred and fifty years before, Dante and Petrarch had begun modern literature, but in France the horrors of the long war with England, of the plague, of the Jacquerie, above all of the civil war, had brutalised men. The ghastly idea of possession by the devil had taken hold of men's minds, and religion became a mockery in the face of the orgies of the Papacy of Avignon or of the monks nearer home.

Born in a time wherein nothing was finished and everything had begun, Louis partook of the monstrous nature of his unformed age, an age in which the 300 registers of the "Trésor des Chartes" paint manners as Villon, Basselin, or Regnier paint them, without shame and without restraint. They show us the bourgeoisie "sans chemise, sans pudeur, et par le dos," as Michelet says, who has so clearly painted the horrors of this age of "lead and iron," from 1300 to 1500.

The policy of centralisation which one day should be the salvation of France was temporarily its ruin; men were reduced to one dull, dead level, the springs of morality were choked, energy was crushed, and when the King wished to rule he found his kingdom little better than an empty void. Thus is it that great discoveries and new inventions, material aid or chance assistance, all do nothing. Yet Joan of Arc had not died or the great chancellor Gerson preached in vain. National life was becoming conscious and active, and under the dead level of administrative uniformity made by Louis, was developing that vigour of intellectual and commercial life which two centuries of misrule from Valois and Bourbon could scarcely crush.

# CHAPTER VIII

## LOCHES (*Continued*)

Sous peu nous détruirons ces hautes
Murailles, briserons ces chaines, et
ferons disparaître ces tortures inventées
par les Rois—trop faibles pour
arréter un peuple qui veut sa
1785 liberté 1785.

*The last Inscription in the prisons of Loches.*[1]

THE great keep built by the Black Count was first used as a prison by that Fulk Rechin whose cruelty had shown itself at Chinon by the lifelong imprisonment of his brother. Passing from these enormous ruins the traveller is led through the chamber where the archers of the Scottish Guard reposed, and is shown what purported to be their ancient beds, structures in solidly-hewn wood, much resembling the accommodation given nowadays to a pack of

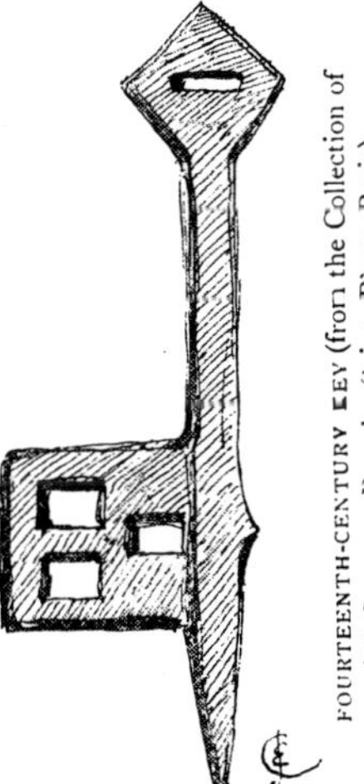

FOURTEENTH-CENTURY KEY (from the Collection of M. Lacoste, Rue des Saints Pères, Paris).

[1] The greater number of the inscriptions mentioned in this chapter

staghounds. The work known as "la Tour Neuve," at the north-west angle of the fortress, was built by Louis XI. less for the sake of increasing the strength of the fortifications than for the security of prisoners. Within a lower room is the torture chamber, with a suggestive-looking iron bar, whose uses the guide will describe with much feeling and expression. We found the place now served as a prison for the Government, but it was empty at the time. Criminals may have been scared at the prospect of a lengthy sojourn in a chamber full of such hideous associations.

"Entrez Messieurs," says an ironical inscription scratched upon the prison walls, "Entrez Messieurs ches le Roy nostre maistre." A cruel King and a hard-hearted when crossed in his desires was the master of Jean Balue, whose cell is in the inner prisons on the second story from the bottom. From the doorway, opening half-way up the wall, we can stand where Louis XI. and his "compère Tristan l'Hermite" stood to watch their wretched prisoner in his cage of iron, whose staples are still fixed into the roof above. It seems almost incredible that western civilisation should have produced a parallel to the hideous sufferings of the caged-in Bajazet at the hands of Tamburlaine ; but

are quoted from the careful copies made by Mrs. Watts Jones, and published by her as "Thoughts in Prison" in the *English Illustrated Magazine* for February 1891.

if the witness of Commines were not enough, there is distinct mention of the making of this very cage in the accounts of Louis XI.[1]

Jean Balue, who from the post of secretary to the King had risen by unscrupulous dishonesty and the omnivorous activity of a reckless parvenu, to the dignity of Bishop of Angers and Cardinal, had rapidly got into the good graces of his master, who seldom asked questions when the ends he wished were attained. At last the schemer overreached himself. After having been responsible for much that happened at Peronne, and gone farther than his powers justified in meddling with the politics of Burgundy, he found it advisable for his own ends, after Louis' return, to sow discord afresh among the royal princes and write treasonable proposals to the Duke of Burgundy.[2] He was imprisoned at Loches, Montbazon, Plessis-lez-Tours, and other places for some eleven years, and died after his release still plotting (with Cardinal de la Rovere) at Ancona.

Another inscription, carved with great care and delicacy in the hard stone, is attributed to a worthier prisoner. The words " Dixisse me aliquando penituit, tacuisse nunquam " may well have been actually

[1] " À Guion de Bue . . . la somme de 60 livres turnois, pour icelle estre par lui employée à faire faire une cage de fer, pour la surreté et garde de la personne du Cardinal d'Angiers."

[2] Jean de Troyes (*Livre des faits advenus au temps du roi Louis XI.*), ". . . et autres grandes et merveilleuses diableries qu'il écrivait audit duc de Bourgogne par un sien serviteur, qui de ces dites lettres et instructions qu'il portait fut trouvé saisi." . . .

traced by the historian-philosopher Commines, who was not only imprisoned but confined in a cage as well. He has described these cages as made "of iron and some of wood, covered with iron plates without and within, 'avec terribles ferrures,' some eight feet broad and about the height of a man. . . . Plusieurs l'ont maudit, et moi aussi qui en ai tâté, sous le roi de présent (Charles VIII.) l'espace de huit mois." He had been implicated in the conspiracy of Orleans in Brittany and elsewhere against the Regent Anne de Beaujeu, of which we have heard already ; and it is strange to think of him sitting within these darkened walls and choosing the phrases for his Chronicles of Louis XI. that were to form the first part of his famous history.

Memories of even more stirring deeds, beneath a brighter sky, were to come to another famous prisoner later on, in whose ears Dante's words were ringing—

"Nessun maggior dolore
Che ricordarsi del tempo felice
Nella miseria."

The inscription that translates this is attributed to Ludovico Sforza, whose dungeon is at the end of interminable passages and dank labyrinths of rock within the foundations of a third tower across the courtyard begun by Louis XI., of which only the Salle des Gardes of Louis XII. now remains above ground.

Our descent "in infernos" now began. Within a little doorway the woman who guided us was striving to light a small and sputtering lamp that seemed to resent being compelled to show off these subterranean mysteries. A narrow twisting staircase leads down to the level of the moat outside, barred with great doors at every turn.

A hundred steps below ground is the cell of Ludovico Sforza, called Il Moro, Duke of Milan. On the wall opposite the window, which gathers through a slit in fourteen feet of rock what little light has strayed into the shadowy passages from the sunny fields of Touraine above, is a small square scratched on the stone to mark the only spot touched by the daylight. The room is also strangely decorated with rough attempts at fresco, with which the prisoner amused himself, red stars in patterns on the wall, and, twice repeated, a prodigious helmet with its casque just showing a stern, hard-looking face inside.[1]

These were but poor substitutes for the fresh frescoes of Leonardo in the beautiful Milan that Sforza was trying to forget, a Milan untouched by time and still enriched with statues that are lost to

[1] The face upon the walls of Loches is not unlike the features of Il Moro in Paulus Jovius, if we take into consideration the difference in training and circumstances of their artists. A much exaggerated account of Ludovico's hardships is given by Jovius, and the interesting fact mentioned of a certain faithful "Pontremulo" having accompanied Sforza in his captivity.

us, with carving still clear and delicate upon its palaces that echoed with the songs of singers from beyond the Alps.

Banished in 1476 by Cecco Simonetta, the Secretary of Galeazzo Maria, Ludovico came back to the imprudent widow Bonne de Savoie, and was accompanied in the darkness of the night by a certain Captain Roberti di Sanseverino. By the next year Cecco was beheaded, as he had prophesied, and Il Moro's little nephews were safely gratifying their tastes for military architecture within the strong walls of the Rocca.

For some time the Regent lived in happiness and great splendour, encouraging the lectures upon science and the classics that learned Greeks or Orientals were giving in Milan ; watching, too, the gallantry and love-making that flourished among his courtiers under his princely rule. And it was from women that his first troubles came. At last he had been obliged to marry his long-imprisoned nephew to Isabel of Arragon—he had himself wedded another princess of Arragon, Beatrice d'Este, the daughter of the Duke of Ferrara, and the women soon began to quarrel. The young Duchess summoned the help of Naples against Ludovico, who then armed himself with letters from the Emperor, and called in Charles VIII. of France, as we have heard before. The opportune death of the young duke left Il Moro with only the infant heir to crush, and his ambitious schemes were prospering, crossed only by the first phenomenal successes of the young French King; but these were soon counterbalanced by the mistakes of Orleans, whose claim to Milan—a fountain of wealth to its possessor in the midst of its rich plain—grew weaker and weaker before the bold policy of Ludovico; for while the widowed Duchess Mabel could get no help from any Court in Italy or out of it, Beatrice d'Este was entertaining the Emperor Maximilian, at the cost of terrible taxation to the Milanese and of her own life to her husband. Her tomb is in the Certosa near Pavia, and close by it is the man who worked through good and evil for her sake, Il Moro, "with the fat face and fine chin of the elderly Napoleon, the beak-like nose of Wellington, a small, querulous, neat-lipped mouth, and immense eyebrows stretched like the talons of an eagle across the low forehead."[1]

But in 1499 the claims of Orleans had become the claims of France. The quarrel for the succession of Milan had become a question of European politics. Louis had conquered Lombardy, and secured new letters from the Emperor to annul Il Moro's claim; and Ludovico himself, "with two small children and some two thousand horse," escaped to Coni, a town upon the route to Germany, exclaiming against the treachery of Venice, yet not strong enough to come to blows with France, "comme tourmenté de peine

[1] Mary Darmesteter, *End of the Middle Ages*, p. 307.

mentale, à voix désolée et regard éploré," as Jean d'Auton tells us. But he had by no means despaired. Sheltered by the King of France's enemy, the Emperor Maximilian of Austria, and provided with "force ducats, qui est une très bonne provision," says Saint Gelais, he managed by the next year to get together sufficient forces of Swiss and others to make another bid for Milan "un morceau si friand et de si bonne digestion." He was helped, too, by the misgovernment of Trivulzio, whom King Louis had left in power, and by the readiness of Milan and the Lombards to revolt, who were "swollen with poison," says the French chronicler, using a metaphor that seems an easy one to writers upon Italy, "and like vipers, ready to secretly shoot forth the venom of their treason." Ludovico Sforza himself, in the age of the Borgias, had not shed so much blood as many of his contemporaries, nay, he had been the patron of literature and art in Milan, yet the fickle Italians had at first welcomed Louis XII.'s army; the change had only come when the alliance with Cæsar Borgia had appeared in all its horror. At this juncture Ludovico returned with an army behind him, swept back Trivulzio from Milan, and took the famous Bayard prisoner. "The Loyal Servitor" tells the story, which does nothing but credit to Il Moro.[1]

[1] See "Le loyal Serviteur," *Chronique du bon Chevalier*, Michaud et Poujoulat, 1re Série, t. iv.

Bayard, being in garrison about twenty miles from Milan, heard that there were some three hundred Italian heads to be broken in Binasco. Now the captain of that place, Messire Jean Bernardin Cazache, being a good knight and well trained in war, did not wait to be taken like a bird upon its nest, but sallied forth valiantly against the small handful of French knights. With loud cries of "France, France! More, More!" the troops met, and the Italians were soon flying towards Milan with Bayard hard upon their tracks. So heartily did the good Chevalier pursue his enemies that, paying no heed to the turning back of his companions, he rushed through the gates of Milan with Cazache's men, and was therein taken and brought before Ludovico, who wondered to see him so young, and asked the business that brought him, in such hurried fashion, to Milan. Bayard, "qui ne fut de rien ébahi," answered courteously and well; and in a short time upon his own good horse again, and clad in the armour he had worn in the pursuit, he was riding out of Milan with a herald and telling the Seigneur de Ligny in the French camp of the courtesy and courage of Il Moro, "qui pour peu de chose n'est pas aisé à étonner."

As we have seen before, Novara stood or fell with Milan, and to the strengthening of Novara Ludovico now turned. Soon after Bayard's adventure La Trémouille and Georges d'Amboise had brought a large body of Swiss and French to the help of Trivulzio at Mortara, and the whole were soon blockading Sforza in the same town in which he had besieged the Duke of Orleans years before.[1]

Ludovico's mercenaries failed him at the crisis, and betrayed him to the French,[2] who put him for safety into the castle of Novara.[3] The King was at Lyons when the news reached him, and Saint Gelais reports the joy with which he announced the taking of Sforza to Anne de Bretagne, comparing La Trémouille to Scipio, Clovis, Charles Martel, and many other military heroes who had deserved well of their country.

The Comte de Ligny himself had recognised the importance of his capture at the moment, and Louis XII. determined to make sure that Ludovico should trouble Italian politics no more. After so many changes came the last scene of all, the beginning of the end. "An old French street surging with an eager mob, through which there jostles a long line

[1] There is a translation of Commines (who is the authority for operations in Italy previous to the taking of Ludovico) made by Thomas Danett in 1596, in which Trivulzio is called "Mr. John James of Trevol." The whole book is almost as good a piece of work as Florio's *Montaigne*, and well worth reading.

[2] He was trying to get away with "ses cheveux troussés sous une coiffe, une gorgerette autour du col, un pourpoint de satin cramoisi, et des chausses d'écarlate, la hallebarde au poing ; et en ce point le prit le Comte de Ligny."—*Jean d'Auton.*

[3] There were Swiss on both sides, but the French recruiting had been done under the authority of the Cantonal administration, and Sforza's Swiss were afraid to oppose them.

of guards and archers; in their midst a tall man, dressed in black camlet, seated on a mule. In his hands he holds his biretta and lifts up unshaded his pale courageous face, showing in all his bearing a great contempt of death. It is Ludovico, Duke of Milan, riding to his cage at Loches." Abbés and scribes of later days who never fought or loved a single hour as Sforza did through all his throbbing, reckless life, have pointed out what consolation it must have afforded to the prisoner to have thus covered his walls with decoration, by the help of necessary ladders too, and even paint-brushes, unwonted solace of a captive's weariness; they forget the inscriptions that run round the walls as well, they forget how bitterly Ludovico found that

> "This is truth the poet sings,
> That a sorrow's crown of sorrow is remembering happier things."

Here for nearly nine years Sforza languished, trying to forget, until he was moved higher up the tower and even allowed some exercise in open air before his death.[1]

[1] The inscriptions Sforza left tell their own pitiful tale of the strong man, who would have welcomed sudden death in fair fight, slowly decaying in this living tomb, where "death assailed him but he could not die."

> "Quant mort me assault et que je ne puis mourir
> Et secourir on ne me veult mais me faire rudesse
> Et de liesse me voir bannir."

And again in large letters among the rough red frescoes—

"Je porte en prison pour ma device que je m'arme de patience par force de peine l'on me fait pouster" (*sic*).

"Ludovico Sforza was called Il Moro," says Jovius, "because he bore

Farther along the same dark passage which opens into Sforza's cell, and deeper still within the earth, is what is known as the Prison of the Bishops. As Il Moro had scratched his spot of sun, so these ecclesiastics had made a pitiful representation of an altar and a cross; and on the wall beneath the window are the marks still left where each in turn gripped the hard stones with his feet and climbed up painfully to see what little light by some mistake had been allowed to shine upon them. Few things in all this miserable mass of terrible recollections seemed to give me so keen a picture of the sufferings endured by men thus shut out from the common air and light of day, as these few poor footsteps so wearily worn out in the hard rock. These prisoners were the Bishops of Puy and Autun,[1] who were implicated in the conspiracy of the Constable Charles de

a mulberry tree for his device, which from the seasons of its flowers and fruit was taken as an emblem of prudence." "God and Il Moro alone know" ran the proverb at the time. Some derive the name wrongly from his dark (Moorish) complexion.

[1] Such is the accepted tradition at the present day. These particular bishops were certainly imprisoned at Loches under the circumstances mentioned above.

In the *Mémoires* of Guillaume de Jaligny (secretary of Pierre de Beaujeu) we hear that in January 1487 the Bishops of Périgueux, called De Pompadour, and of Montauban, called De Chaumont, were found in correspondence with Dunois and Orleans in the same plot in which Commines was implicated, and which led to the war in Brittany. "Pour ce sujet," says Jaligny, "le roi les fit un matin constituer prisonniers," and they were interrogated before the officers of the Archbishop of Tours. So this same cell may have acquired an "odour of sanctity" even before the conspiracy of Bourbon in 1523.

Bourbon, just before the defeat of Francis I. at Pavia.

Bourbon, who at the time of his marriage was the most powerful prince in France, was relentlessly attacked after his wife's death by the wicked and avaricious Louise de Savoie. By the aid of her execrable tool, the Chancellor Du Prat, she finally drove him out of the kingdom, threw one of the French King's strongest nobles into the arms of the Emperor, and was responsible for a career of lawlessness and rapine which ended in the sack of Rome. But Bourbon, before he became merely a reckless adventurer, had aimed at forming for himself a kingdom of his vast possessions in the heart of France, backed by the forces of the Emperor, and with England in her old provinces to the south. It was in this part of the conspiracy that the bishops with whom we are concerned were implicated, and they certainly suffered to the full the penalty for their imprudence. Bourbon's secret negotiations with the Emperor had taken place in the spring of 1523, and though rumours of them had reached the Court, Francis had paid no attention to them, and was on his way to Lyons for the march that was to end in Pavia, when the Sieur de Brézé, Seneschal of Normandy, husband of the famous Diana, brought him accurate tidings of the conspiracy, which were obtained through the confession of two Norman gentlemen—De Brézé had no notion that he was implicating in this terrible charge his own wife's father, Jean de Poitiers, Seigneur de Saint Vallier. After this warning the King waited for further reinforcements at Moulins, and there met Bourbon, who pretended to be ill and would not see him, fearing that the evil influence of Louise de Savoie would overcome the natural generosity of Francis.

In a few days Bourbon escaped to his fortified castle of Chantelles, and from there sent the Bishop of Autun to the King asking for assurances of restitution to his lands and goods. But the King's deepest suspicions had been aroused by the flight, and the bishop was arrested on his way to Lyons, bearing the Constable's despatches, and with him Saint Vallier, Émard de Prie, La Vauguyon, and others of the duke's friends. Bourbon meanwhile went on, stopping for one night at Puy in Auvergne, probably with his friend the bishop, and at length after several exciting escapes got safe to Italy.

Still deeper in the hideous recesses of the rock of Loches, in gloomy caverns where the light from our small lamp could barely penetrate to the fungus rotting on the slimy walls, is the den where Saint Vallier, the father of Diane de Poitiers, was shut up by Francis I. "Monsieur mon fils," he writes to his son the Seneschal, "le Roy m'a faict prendre sans nulle raison . . et m'a faict mener icy au chasteau de Loches comme un faulx traistre qui m'est si très horrible regret que je m'en meurs." And to Diana: "Madame—suis icy arrivé au chasteau de Loches aussy mal traicté que paouvre prisonnier pourroit estre . . . je vous requiers ayez tant de pityé de vostre paouvre père que de le vouloir venir veoir."[1] And Diana did her best, though at first with little success, for the King wrote hotly to his judges to press the trial, and to find out by any and every means, from Saint Vallier and the others, all the details of the conspiracy. "Il faut nécessairement et promptement sçavoir," he writes, "au besoin par torture qui sont les conspirateurs. . . . Saint Vallier et d'Escar savent tout."[2] Sentence of death was with difficulty remitted to imprisonment for life. "Entre quatre murailles de pierre maçonnées dessus et dessous, es quelles n'y aura qu'une petite fenestre."[3] It is said that at last Diana's entreaties won her father's freedom from the King, and it adds another memory to these strange dungeons to think of Diana picking her way through the black passages towards the cell where her father lay waiting his deliverance, his hair turned white with the horror of thick darkness round him. Far longer is the tale of the prisoners of Loches—

[1] MS. Fr., No. 5109, fos. 103, 104.

[2] MS. Fr., No. 5109, fo. 111.

[3] In 1525 the Constable Bourbon expressly stipulates, in his treaty with the King of Spain, for the deliverance of Saint Vallier, so he must have been in prison at least two years. For the conspiracy of Bourbon see Du Bellay, xvii., 266, etc., Belleforest, ii. 1434, etc.

"Qui no sab de sospirar
Vinga sen assi estar,
Car no sol sospirara
Mas de dolar gemira,"[1]

wrote one of them in the cachot of the drawbridge, and I can imagine no place so full of terrible associations; but only a few of the most important have been spoken of here. Among later prisoners was Charles de Lorraine, Duc d'Elbœuf, a man of little merit, who fell with the rest of the house of Guise after the murders at Blois. De Retz has summed him up in a few bitter sentences as a man without heart and without intelligence—"c'était le galimatias du monde le plus fleuri"—who lost his nobility of character with his riches, and forfeited every claim to pity in misfortune.

More worthy of commiseration, if not more unhappy, was François de Rochechouart, nephew of the Cardinal de la Rochefoucauld, who was implicated in the various miserable Court intrigues of "Monsieur" in 1633. For two years he was kept in the walls of Loches by Richelieu, without any positive proof having been brought against him, and merely in the hope of extracting some confession from his misery. To the same end he was ordered for execution and reprieved at the last moment, but

[1] Mrs. Watts Jones gives the following translation of the above—

"He who sighs hath never known,
Come within these walls of stone;
Here not only shall he sigh,
He shall groan in misery."

nothing would shake his determination to keep silence, and he finally left France for Italy until the King's death. No wonder that amid so many gruesome realities one fable has arisen that has even received the support of serious authorities. A certain Pontbrillant, Governor of Loches, had the unpleasant curiosity to investigate the inmost recesses of its prisons. Several iron doors were broken down, and at last behind one of them was found the body of a man sitting with his head upon his hands, of great stature, and clothed like a knight of three centuries ago. The corpse fell into dust on contact with the outer air. Here is much matter for a tragedy. But what is known and certain is sadder than any imagination, and nothing in the castle leaves so deep an impression as the scratches and lines upon the walls with which the prisoners strove to lighten the weariness of their cells or to keep some thought of hope within their hearts. Here is one more of these inscriptions, with whose graceful sentiment we left behind us the blackened walls of Loches—

> "Qui vaut mieux amour ou justice ?
> Et se tousiours amour estoit
> Da point justice ne faudroit
> Pour ce que amour est follie
> Et loin justice establie, Responce
> Amour vaut mieux."

# CHAPTER IX

## LANGEAIS

> " Anne, qui fut femme de deux grands rois ;
> En tout grande cent fois, comme reine deux fois.
> Jamais reyne comme elle n'enrichit tant la France,
> Voylà que c'est d'avoir une grande alliance."
>
> BRANTÔME, *Anne de Bretagne.*

WE had already heard much of Anne de Bretagne in the course of our wanderings along the Loire, and after seeing her oratory at Loches it became impossible to put off any longer a visit to the hall where she was married in Langeais. The road from Tours to Langeais is a straight and good one, whether for riding or driving, and follows the right or north bank of the river past Luynes to Cinq Mars, where the railway crosses over too, and follows the road [1] into Langeais between the river and a hill upon its banks.

The village at first sight does not look attractive,

[1] The high road from Paris to Angers.

but there is one good main street, from which numberless little alleys open out lined by tiny cottages, and ending in a strip of green or garden ground. At the end of this street rise two vast round towers that from a distance look far too big for their surroundings, and it is not till the visitor is fairly in the little square beyond the house of Rabelais, and face to face with the main entrance, that he can realise the full proportions of the Château of Langeais.

Alingavia, says M. Mabille, was one of the oldest of the Roman settlements, and Roman remains are still traceable in the foundations of the old donjon keep, rebuilt in 1000. Gregory of Tours tells us, too, that St. Martin built a church here, and the present edifice contains some of the early work near the east end, which is triapsal ;[1] some old shafts and arches are arranged on the south side so as to form a covered walk externally.[2]

But of the buildings within the castle walls, of which distinct traces are still left, the fort built by Foulques Nerra to blockade Eudes at Tours is the oldest. Little but the outer shell of its walls and a few traces of masonry about the windows remains, but from the little hill on which it stands can be obtained the finest view of the inner side of the château. "The interior court" — I quote from Mrs. Mark

[1] Henry Petit, *op. cit.*

[2] In 1118 the Fulk of Anjou who died upon the throne of Jerusalem in 1142, built a chapel at Langeais, and founded a collegiate church for his relics from Palestine.

Pattison [1]—"is almost wholly confined by the buildings around it; the high walls which defend it on the outside are cut up at well-guarded angles by massive towers, and pierced at irregular intervals by narrow openings. The whole length is crowned by heavy machicolated battlements, so that the aspect of the exterior is severe, but the façade which looks upon the court is not wanting in elegance. Four small towers, each of which contains a spiral staircase, break the monotony of the front and give access to the different stories. The interior space is divided out in the simplest fashion, and the arrangements adopted on the ground floor continue in unvarying repetition tier above tier. But above, along the roof, run no heavy battlements; a bold projecting cornice takes their place in surmounting the wall, and over this rises a sharply pointed roof, the outline of which is broken by towers and pierced by chimneys and dormers."

I have quoted thus far to make quite clear the exact position of Langeais in the architecture of Touraine. It is a fortress of the Middle Ages that is one of the finest existing examples of a French castle built about the middle of the fifteenth century, and bears upon its very walls the traces of coming change. The cornice, which at Langeais replaces the battlements on the walls of the inside only, is destined soon to replace them on the outside also.

[1] *The Renaissance of Art in France*, vol. i. cap. 2.

"At Chenonceaux, at Azay-le-Rideau, at Blois, at Chambord, its bold projecting lines encircle each building with a crown." We had seen the older forms of feudal architecture at Chinon and at Loches; Langeais seemed the connecting link between the older order and the new. The problem which its architect had to solve was to combine a stronghold capable of defence with a house calculated for the increasing necessities of daily life; the fortifications seem planned on a scale very much behind the science of the times, for gunpowder is left wholly out of the calculation, while every means for keeping out an escalade attack has been carefully made use of: the only gate that opens from without into the court is flanked, as at Chaumont, by two massive towers and guarded by a portcullis.

Of the first building on this site, after the Black Count's donjon had fallen into ruins, little save a few bricks remains to indicate that Romano-Gallic methods of construction still continued. A later château was begun by Pierre de la Brosse, the son of a good family in Touraine, who had seen some service in the Court of St. Louis, and reached the highest powers of a favourite under Philip III. Against all the enemies whom such a position naturally aroused Pierre was able to make a good resistance until he imprudently attacked the reputation of the Queen, who joined the barons against him and finally hanged him at Vincennes in

1272, on charges which have remained unknown and were probably designedly obscured.

It is this same old château which was occupied by the English during their invasions while the Black Prince was making his campaign along the Loire; it was given up to Charles VII. only to

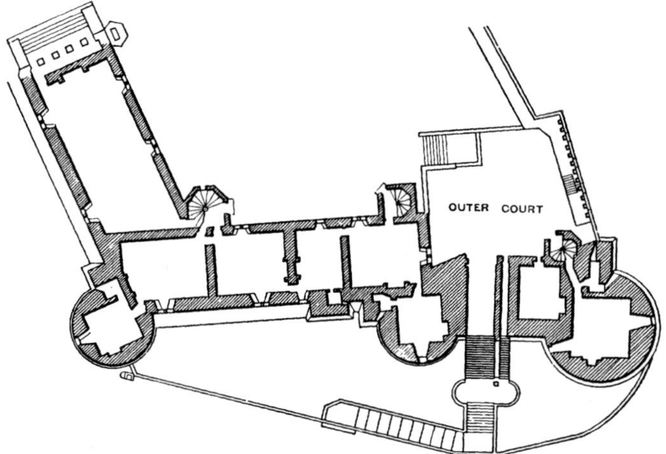


PLAN OF LANGEAIS (drawn by Roy in *Langeais*, by M. Brincourt).

be retaken, and at last the English were bought out of Langeais as they were out of Rochecorbon by the combined subsidies of the citizens of Touraine.

The Château of Langeais as it stands at present was built in 1464 under the direction of Jean Briçonnet, first mayor of Tours, by the care of Jean Bourrée, minister of Louis XI., and governor of Langeais, who was also the builder of Plessis-lez Tours, a château which in its complete state wa very like what Langeais has remained. The place is now in the possession of M. Siefried, and, by his judicious and tasteful expenditure of large sums of money, is being gradually brought into one harmonious picture of oak carvings, tapestry, and warm tiled floors—the chimney and ceiling of the Salle des Gardes are especially beautiful ; its walls are painted by Lameire with the arms of Anne de Bretagne, whose cordelière reappears in many other details of the decoration.

Perhaps the strangest feature of the place is the quaint little passage beneath the roof, the guards' "chemin de ronde," formed by the machicolations, that extends all round the château, lighted by innumerable little windows which give an ever-changing view of the valley of the Loire from the forest of Chinon west and south, to the cathedral towers of Tours far off among the mist towards the east. But the most interesting room in Langeais is the great hall, where Anne de Bretagne was married to King Charles VIII. of France.

The story of the war in Brittany, and the revolt of Orleans against the Regent Anne de Beaujeu, has already introduced us to the little Breton duchess. Brantôme sketches her portrait in his Gallery of Illustrious Ladies. "Her figure," says he, "was small and delicate. It is true that one leg was shorter than the other, though by very little, and it was scarcely noticeable, for her beauty was no whit damaged by that, and many very beautiful women have I noticed with this same slight defect (*ceste legère défectuosité*), such as the Duchesse de Longueville. Besides, there would seem to be a great fascination about the walk of such women, owing to

ANNE DE BRETAGNE.

certain graces of movement which are not commonly found in others."[1] Add to this a calm and dignified carriage, which revealed the firm will and resolution of character ripened at an early age by the troubles of the times. But if Anne had thus far gained from her Breton upbringing, she had all the Breton faults,

[1] The firm chin and somewhat large nose of her face in later life are best seen in the medal struck in 1499, after her second marriage, which bears the legend "Lugdun · Republica · gaudente · Bis ·Anna · regnante benigne · sic · fui · conflata.

the pride, the anger, and the self-will of that strong and narrowed nationality. If her wishes were clearly defined, her will imperious, her views were also somewhat limited : she lacked the supple nature of a truly great woman, because she was without that loftiness of mind and intellect which allows its possessor to appreciate while it criticises every form of life and manners with which it comes in contact. This is why we find her alternately the prey to pride, to anger, and to hate, to a tenacity of purpose through good and evil which degenerates into a wrong-headed sullenness. "Once she has bethought her of anything," says Contarini, the Venetian ambassador, "she must have her way, whether by smiles or tears." Similarly it is her love of vengeance, her unrelenting hatred, that her panegyrist Brantôme can alone find to blame, "si la vengeance est un sy, puisqu'elle est si belle et si douce." It was she who built the good ship *La Cordelière* which blew up in action with the English fleet off Saint Maché in August 1513.

A princess with so strongly marked a character was not one to let herself be married at the convenience of her subjects or of any man, and all Europe had been already somewhat amused at her capture of the unwilling Maximilian and her alliance with England and Spain. This could have but one result. Anne's new allies were by no means inclined to attach the importance to the Breton duchess which she desired, and France was only made the more attentive to the frontier and the incessant quarrels of the Breton lords. At last the politic and skilful Regent saw her opportunity. Making every use of the influence over Anne possessed by the young Duke of Orleans just released from prison, and tempting at the same time her ambition by the offer of a throne, the Regent arranged the marriage of her young brother Charles VIII. with the heiress of Brittany. The duchess had little scruple in giving up her tardy lover Maximilian, whose daughter had already been somewhat similarly abandoned by the King of France, and in December 1491 the marriage contract of Anne and Charles VIII. was drawn up in the great hall of the Château of Langeais, which assured the union of France and Brittany, and gave the business-like little Breton the right of marrying the next King of France if she outlived her first husband.

At this time she was about seventeen years old. The firmness of her character was yet veiled by the modesty and grace of youth, and all her natural courage and loyalty was conspicuous.

Strictly honourable in her life as she was faithful to her religion, she at once took up the authority of her position and grasped the meaning of affairs around her. Contarini describes her husband at the same period as plain of visage, with great eyes that seemed to see but weakly, an aquiline nose too large for the face, and thick lips always open, slow of speech, and with certain nervous movements in his hands. Beside Charles VIII., among the courtiers in the great hall round her, stands Étienne de Vesc, the historian, talking of the manuscript of Livy, which he had asked La Trémouille to bring back for him from Brittany, and behind him is the Maréchal de Gié, looking somewhat distrustfully at the new Queen, with whom he is no great favourite, and whose bitter hatred he will afterwards incur.

Pierre de Rohan, Sire de Gié, of a Breton stock, had the blood of Du Guesclin in his veins, through his grandfather's marriage, and by his mother was a descendant of the Viscontis. He was taken from Brittany, where his recollections were not of the most pleasant kind,[1] by the Admiral de Montauban, and by him placed in the Court of Louis XI., where he learned to be a good Frenchman even if he were a bad Breton. In six years he was a councillor and captain of the Château of Blois, and, later on, is sent with Commines to Amiens, where negotiations with England were in progress, to see that nothing contrary to agreement was attempted by the crowd of English soldiers who had come with their ambassador. But no especial watchfulness was necessary; the Englishmen were found to be all dead drunk. He was with Commines, too, when Louis was struck

[1] His mother had poisoned his father, her first husband, and died in the dungeon where her second husband cautiously put her.

with apoplexy at Chinon, and his skill in diplomacy and Court affairs is evident from his success in the arrangements made for the government of the kingdom by Charles d'Amboise and the rest in that little room beneath the King's bed, while the terrible patient above was striving not to lose his authority with his failing strength. It is one more proof of his tact that, though a member of the Regent Anne de Beaujeu's council, he could yet remain a firm friend of Louis d'Orléans, calm down the revolts in Brittany, and finally be one of the chief negotiators in the marriage of the Duchess Anne.

De Gié was uneasy, and with reason, at the conversation of the Court. The King, who had grown up neglected at Amboise with nothing to occupy his thoughts but the romances of chivalry which Charlotte de Savoie read him, had only been preserved from hazarding his forces sooner by the interruptions of the war in Brittany. But now great movements seemed to be in the air. In the year after his marriage Spain had chased the Moors from Granada, and America was discovered by Columbus. The full effects of the policy of Louis XI. became evident not only in the pursuance of his Italian schemes, but in the strength and consolidation of the royal power which made such attempts possible at all.

The invasion of Italy had been a constant dream among Frenchmen, and now, amid the confusion of Europe, France saw her opportunity. The Mussulman raids from the East had terribly exhausted life and property in Italy; Venice and Naples had even been so mad as to use these dangerous neighbours against each other, and make a Turkish invasion possible. There was danger, too, from the West. Since 1480 Torquemada had made all Spain like one vast furnace of human flesh, and had turned out the Jews to wander over Europe leaving plague and famine in their tracks; twenty thousand famishing spectres died before the walls of Genoa. Italy herself was filled with prodigies and warnings; men like Machiavelli, in despair of Divine help, had taken Policy for their god, others were listening to the warnings of Savonarola, or watching the pictures full of the sombre teaching of the grief of Michael Angelo.

In the midst of all this the ambition of the young French King, which had been smouldering since the Venetian embassy in 1484, was fanned into quick flame by the messages of Ludovico Sforza—France should step in to this distracted Italy, France who alone could understand the message which Italy had to give, who was to make a discovery more powerful in its results than that of Spain beyond the ocean, and to set in motion the two great electric currents; one, called the Renaissance, setting away from Christianity, the other, called the Reformation, trying to get nearer to it; the school of Rabelais and Voltaire on the one side, the Puritanism of Luther and of Calvin on the other.

Commines tells the whole story of this ill-advised invasion of Italy "without generals, without money, with the impromptu army of a moment's whim." Let us look closer at this strange company that is crossing the passes of the Alps. It is evening, and through the smoky glare of the torches appear the tall halberds of the first division above their waving plumes, a barbarian division of Swiss and German freebooters, tall ruffians in many-coloured tunics short-waisted, with tightly-fitting leggings, and cuirasses only in the front rank; behind them comes the short quick step of the small sunburnt Gascons, some six thousand of them, quick and hot fighters, and the best marching men in Europe; close on their heels are the cavalry in full armour, each horseman accompanied by his page and servants and riding a monstrous charger without tail or ears; these are followed by the light cavalry armed with bows, and by the Scottish guard,[1] behind whom rides the King surrounded by three hundred archers and two hundred picked horsemen clad in gold and scarlet; in the rear are the lumbering uncouth machines that served as cannon; and thus they march on towards the

[1] The Scotch bodyguard at the French Court, says Fleuranges in 1507, wore white jerkins covered with gold embroidery, with a crown on their breasts. In *Some Account of the Stuarts of Aubigny*, Lady Elizabeth Cust has added an important chapter to the interesting story of the Scots in France who had become connected with the most influential families in Europe; both Esmé Stuart, for instance, and his wife, Katherine de Balsac, could trace relationship with the Viscontis of Milan.

unknown country, which will receive them, much to their surprise, as something superhuman and Divine, and suffer itself to be swiftly conquered ; too swiftly to be safely done : but the Alps might now be sunk into the sea—the boast of Cicero was true again though with a changed meaning ; the mountain passes had been often crossed before, but never had so much been carried home again by the returning soldiers.

It was a distracted country this Italy through which the stampede of the young French King's army rushed almost unhindered, a country where Leonardo's frescoes and Bellini's Madonnas looked down upon the crimes of Borgias and the ambitions of the Medicis ; where the burning words of Savonarola taught the people submission to the scourge of God ; where Capponi roused the burghers to enthusiasm for their new French patron, and opposition to young Piero de Medicis, the mortal enemy of France. But Piero had made no plans for defence and no schemes for alliance, and found himself at last obliged to leave his Florentine palace and his young son Lorenzo (the father of Catherine de Medicis) and meet the French King in his camp. There was a great contrast in the two men : the handsome, graceful Italian, arrogant and proud as he was cruel, and the small, high-shouldered Frenchman looking sickly and but half grown up, yet with the bright eyes that promised a kindly, honest nature, and a power over his soldiery that sent them to the death in fighting for his sake.

A third contrast was added by the presence of Ludovico Sforza, who was already beginning to be perplexed at the young King's success, and now found that Charles had completely outwitted the Florentine and secured all the best side of the bargain for Italian lands and money.

In November 1494 the French troops were marching through the streets of Pisa, gay with decorations and crowded with a wildly enthusiastic populace, crying "Liberté, Liberté," and casting down the great lion that represented the hated Signorie of Florence from its pillar over the bridge of Arno; in a few days the King's statue was there in its place; "but," says Commines, "they have since done with the King as they did with the lion, for it is the nature of the Italians to do pleasure to the strongest, though these Pisans had received such harsh treatment (from Florence) that they may be excused." Charles himself was compelled by circumstances stronger than his inclinations to behave with little kindness to this harassed town of Pisa. No sooner had he left the town upon his way to Florence, than the impossibility of his promises became clear—to support Pisa was to give deadly offence to Florence, for, says Commines, "Pise leur est plus grande chose que Florence propre, sauf les corps et les meubles."

But the young King was too much the slave of his first honest impulses to thrive in the land of Machiavelli; he could not see much farther than the successes of the present. The whole expedition was equally uncertain in its movements and its aims; triumphal entries into Naples, Florence, even Rome itself, availed nothing; the advice of Briçonnet and De Vesc weighed as little with the young King as did the more prudent counsels of Commines or the Maréchal de Gié, and when the great league against the French with Venice at its head became a fact accomplished, there was nothing for it but retreat which all but ended in disaster.

The army had made another Capua of Naples and delayed the homeward march too long; it was stayed still further by the attractions of the Pisan ladies, and now Louis d'Orléans was blockaded in Novara. At last they were caught by the enemy at the foot of the Apennines, and death stared them in the face. "La peur," says Commines, "venait aux plus braves." Then De Gié with Jean Jacques Trivulzio and a handful of men took Pontremoli, crossed the steep pass and came down near Fornova close to the enemy, who were camped by the river Taro, swollen with floods. While De Gié with difficulty held his dangerous position between the river and the hill, the French army laboriously climbed the same slopes he had crossed before, and for six days with bleeding hands dragged their cannon and their baggage across the pitiless rocks, in danger all the time of being cut to pieces by the enemy's attack. But the Italians waited; the Bishop of St. Malo and Philippe de Commines tried negotiations, but they failed, and the fight soon began. The King rode at the head of his troops and showed himself as brave as any of his men, and though fighting one against six the French at last cut their way through with the loss of some two hundred men against four thousand of the enemy.

Even then the advice of the more prudent was rejected; the Breton commanders and St. Malo would not recognise that there was nothing left but an honourable retreat; it was only the terrible news that kept pouring into the camp from all sides that at last decided Charles to advance towards rest and help at Asti and Turin. A peace was patched up hastily, chiefly through the negotiations of Commines, and the King got back to Lyons, where after two months came the news of the death of the little Dauphin, whose tomb is in the cathedral of Tours. This sorrow seems to have been far more bitterly felt by the mother than by Charles, and Anne's feelings were still further hurt by the ill-restrained joy of Louis d'Orléans, who felt himself a step nearer to the throne of France.[1]

[1] Commines relates how, with a strange idea of lightening the sorrows of the Queen, Charles had in several young courtiers to dance before her, "et entre les autres y était le duc d'Orléans qui pouvait bien avoir trente quatre ans." The duke seems to have put more joy than sympathy into these ill-timed capers.

An unusual reason is given for Charles's own lack of sympathy—"ledit Dauphin," continues the same authority, "avait environ trois ans, bel enfant et audacieux en parole;" and the little King seems to

TOMB OF THE CHILDREN OF CHARLES VIII. AND ANNE OF BRITTANY (carved by Jean Juste).

In April 1498 the King died suddenly at Amboise, in the same spring which saw the martyrdom of Savonarola, and Anne de Bretagne became for a short time a widow.

Langeais seems to have justified its existence by providing a shelter for the Breton Queen, and neither before nor after that event is there much of interest or importance in its history. But before bidding it farewell there is one more memory, a very different one, that cannot but detain a traveller in the land of Rabelais.

In 1534 the chronicler of the *Heroic Deeds of Pantagruel* was in Rome with Du Bellay, and for the next ten years remained under the protection of that house, until the death of Du Bellay, "Sieur de Langey," in 1543. We can imagine the laughter that rang through the halls of Langeais as the jovial doctor discoursed with his patron of the customs of Paris and of Rome; what would not any of us give for an hour's such talk with Rabelais? Of the four great French prose writers of the sixteenth century, says Sainte-Beuve, Rabelais remains more popular than Calvin or than Amyot, more amusing than Montaigne; nor should we see by the chimney corner at Langeais a man such as Rabelais paints himself in his book; we should see a man of science

have feared comparison with his own shortcomings; "mais était si bon, qu'il n'est possible de voir meilleur créature." Even in an attempt at censure Commines cannot withhold his liking for the honest, ugly Charles.

and of study, a man of good company above all, of jests and jokes incomparable. Many have admired Rabelais without appreciating him, more still have read into his honest satire opinions that he never meant, and doctrines that suited the leanings of his critics; he has been called the precursor of the Revolution, the apostle of humanitarianism, by an age that thought it honoured him in the appellation, but he was neither; he was but the frank, outspoken critic of his time, a man who wrote and spoke for men in a rougher and less fastidious age than ours. "A nation should always possess one such man," says Sainte-Beuve, "but more than one is dangerous."

Langeais was troubled, we have it on the authority of Pantagruel, at the passing of "the generous and heroic soul of the learned Chevalier de Langey." "Il m'en souvient (dist Epistemon) et encore me frissonne et tremble le cœur dedans sa capsule, quand je pense es prodiges tant divers et horrificques." His friends and servants all in terror looked on one another in silence, without a word for the thoughts that were within them of the loss to the glory and safety of France in so perfect and good a knight. Let any one read this chapter in the Fourth Book, and the next one telling of the loud voice that called across the silence of the sea from Paxos, and cried to the sailors of Epitherses, "Pan, the great god, is dead." Let any one read these, and he will no

LANGEAIS FROM THE PARK. INTERIOR OF THE COURTYARD.

longer leave his Rabelais to curious scholars, or condemn him as beneath the notice of the virtuous.[1]

In later years Langeais often changed owners. In 1631 it passed from the hands of Louise, daughter of Henri, Duc de Guise, to those of Cinq Mars, Marshal of France, and in 1765 to the Duc de Luynes. After another century of changes it came into the possession of its present owner, M. Siefried. No ancient castle could possess a better châtelain ; all its old beauties are preserved, and the necessities of a more complex modern life are introduced with a care and an artistic feeling that leave no sense of incongruity or incompleteness. Nor are the charms of Langeais limited to its castle walls. The park that stretches out upon the hill behind the donjon of Foulques Nerra is as full of beauty of its own kind as the château. As we wandered through it on a day whose sudden showers made every gleam of sunshine lovelier, we passed several caves in the soft rock by the side of the winding road, which might have been the traces of a subterranean passage, and finally stopped where the path through tangled trees led to a little knoll crowned by a pillar with an eagle on its capital ; from here there is a fine view of the windings of the Loire and the pretty little suspension bridge that leads to Candes and

[1] For the "dernier mot" on Rabelais and the hitherto unknown Bernard Salignac to whom he attributes all his knowledge, see *Rabelais et son maître*, by Arthur Heulhard, Paris, A. Lemerre.

Anjou, close to where, as Dumas tells us, poor Monsieur Surintendant Fouquet, flying down the stream, became convinced that he was being chased by Colbert in the ugly eight-oared galley that was following him.

The river and its banks are quiet enough now, and as we passed them in the gathering twilight on our way to Tours, the resolute figure of the small Breton Queen came back to us and left a stirring memory of the halls of Langeais.

# CHAPTER X

## CHAUMONT

"Laissez faire à Georges."

CHAUMONT is within a couple of hours' drive from Blois, along the same road that skirts the northern bank of the Loire for some distance both east and west from Tours.

The river flows southward from Blois as far as Chouzy, and then taking a sharp turn to the west passes under the magnificent bridge which connects the villages of Chaumont and Onzain. From this bridge there is one of the finest views, among many, of the sweeping current of the Loire. The forest of Blois, which we had left behind us, just shows above the house-tops, and across the river the towers of the castle rise upon the wooded hill and dominate the little village by the banks.[1]

[1] Evelyn, in 1644, saw this view from another direction scarcely less beautiful.

On 2nd May he writes in the *Diary*: "We took boate, passing by Charmont (*sic*), a proud castle on the left hand; before it is a sweete island deliciously shaded with tall trees."

In the time of the early Angevin Counts, Chaumont was one of the outposts of the Counts of Blois towards their enemies' country, and was given to Gelduin, Lord of Saumur, after Foulques Nerra had so suddenly turned him out of his own castle by the famous night attack, which owed its supernatural swiftness—so men said—to the help of the devil. The son of this Gelduin was the first of that famous family of D'Amboise which was to give so many celebrated names to the history of France, and the Château of Amboise itself seems to have originally formed part of the same estates. But Amboise was too far off from Blois and too near the formidable Counts of Anjou and Touraine to remain in this connection for long; indeed, it was owing to a reverse in one of the perpetual wars with Henry Plantagenet that the first castle at Chaumont was razed to the ground. It was a few years after the new building had arisen that Henry II. met Thomas à Becket here for the last time before the archbishop's murder; and just before it was again completely destroyed there was born here, in 1460, the most famous of his race, Georges, Cardinal d'Amboise.

This second destruction was due to the political blunders of Georges' father, Pierre d'Amboise, who, after assisting Louis XI. as Dauphin in the conspiracies of the Praguerie, was so ill-advised as to oppose that astute monarch later on in the rebellion called the "War of the Public Weal." His punishment, the destruction of his château, suited at once Louis' principles of summary justice and his policy of weakening the nobles on every possible occasion.

But the family of D'Amboise was too powerful to remain long without a home, and in a few years the château which still exists was built at Chaumont by Philibert de l'Orme. It is not a palace, and in comparison with the gigantic bulk of Chambord seems of merely ordinary dimensions, but it is compact and perfect in itself, depending wholly on the corner towers for the necessary amount of "perpendicular accent," and showing very clearly the transition which we had already noticed at Langeais from the fortress to the later château. There are still the two great towers that guard the entrance, and on the left side towards the river another tower, that binds together the corners of the *corps de logis*, rises above the line of roofs, and plunges boldly downwards in one sweeping line through brakes and brambles to the foot of the hill.

The whole château was originally built by Charles, the brother of the Cardinal, who also held high office in the State, in the form of a quadrangle, but the fourth side towards the river, which existed in 1681,[1] was pulled down by M. de Vaugien, a Parisian magistrate, to whom the domain belonged in 1739. The space thus opened out forms a magnificent terrace

[1] Félibien, *Mémoires inédits sur les maisons royales de France.*

looking out upon the Loire and backed by the main buildings of the castle which have lately been restored ; and with De Vigny's help it is quite possible to imagine, behind the broad windows that line the courtyard, the festive Maréchal de Bassompierre entertaining the company with his stories of Henry IV. and the Princess of Condé, while young Cinq Mars, "in a fine melancholy" at the other end of the table, is forgetting his dinner to watch the bright eyes of Marie de Gonzague for the last time before he rides away from Chaumont to the Court.

On the left hand of the entrance gate is the Cardinal's hat and coat-of-arms of Georges d'Amboise, while the porcupine of his master, Louis XII., is on the inside of the wing that joins the entrance towers.

The rise to power of the future favourite was rapid and precocious. At fourteen, when the new Chaumont was scarcely risen from its foundations, young D'Amboise was made Bishop of Montauban, and very soon became the almoner of King Louis XI. in a Court where he would have the best of training in the art of holding his tongue and managing political intrigues expeditiously and quietly. Of this sagacity he soon gave proof. In the conspiracy of Louis d'Orléans against Anne de Beaujeu he was arrested with Commines for complicity in the plot, but by making use of the bold defence that if he had persuaded Charles VIII. to leave the protection of the Regent he had also clearly acted on the express wishes of the King, he met the chief charge of his accusers and escaped the cage and imprisonment from which Commines suffered at Loches.

D'Amboise's connection with the Duke of Orleans was judiciously maintained during the whole of Charles VIII.'s reign, and while Louis was governor of Normandy, D'Amboise, as Archbishop of Rouen, was of material assistance in crushing out the brigandage and violence which were rampant at that time in the north of France. Later on, he was with the duke at Asti and Novara, and supported with his patron the charge of malpractices which was again brought against them on their return from Italy.

In a short time the Duke of Orleans was Louis XII., and Georges d'Amboise found himself one of the chief supporters of the throne of France.

But higher dignities still were to come to D'Amboise from the Italy which had just been somewhat ingloriously left. Amidst the numerous intrigues of the Papal Court, Cæsar Borgia found himself in need of one more dupe, of an instrument by whose means he could influence the powerful Court of France, and whose personal ambition would be served by a closer connection with the politics of Rome; a Briçonnet had already been found,[1] another like him was soon forthcoming; Georges d'Amboise

[1] After D'Amboise's death there is yet another French ecclesiastic who is ready to play the same rôle, the infamous Du Prat, the Chancellor of Louise de Savoie. Biragues, of the St. Bartholomew, is another instance later on.

answered all the requirements of Cæsar Borgia, and to all the daring of Briçonnet he added a greater shrewdness, a more capable intellect, and a more assured position of command. An opportunity soon offered itself for the Papal Court to fulfil its promises.

The unhappy Jeanne de France had from the first been disliked by her husband, and it only needed the touch of pathos which Scott has supplied in the suggestion of her own unrequited passion, to complete a picture of distress and misery rarely found in the story of a French princess. Louis XII., when King, was only too glad to add reasons of State to his own personal repugnance, and with singular brutality[1] to repudiate this faithful and uncomplaining wife. Jeanne died in 1504 at Bourges, and Anne de Bretagne reigned in her stead. It is not impossible that certain recollections of the young duchess during his campaign in Brittany may have come back to Louis after the death of her first husband had given him the throne; in any case the care for her own future which the Breton had shown in the marriage settlement at Langeais now had its result. For the second time Anne was a Queen of France, and for the second time the usual businesslike agreement was drawn up as to her own estates and property — it will be seen that the

[1] Jean Bouchet (*Panégyrique de la Trémouille*) gives a far too flattering account of this transaction; for what actually happened see *Procédures Politiques du règne de Louis XII.* (M. de Maulde), in which is also the Life of the Maréchal de Gié.

strongly-marked characteristics of her earlier years show themselves in a far more decided manner during this second period of her power. Though Anne never really cared for the true interests of France, she was only too glad to join D'Amboise in managing the King, and the bitterness of her disappointment at having no male issue warped her pride and natural tenacity into a fatally misguided policy from which France was only saved by her death.

It was in the preliminaries to this royal marriage that Rome began to show her influence with the Court of France. The papal bull necessary for the King's divorce was brought to Chinon by Cæsar Borgia, and the same hand gave Georges d'Amboise his Cardinal's hat. Michelet, describing the statue on the Cardinal's tomb at Rouen, one of the finest monuments of the time in France, calls it a peasant face ; it is certainly no courtier that kneels there in his flowing robes before the carving of his patron saint slaying the dragon, but it is far more than a peasant : a peculiarly square head, with deep, low eyebrows, long upper lip, heavy jaw, and that firmness of character expressed in every line of bone and muscle which seldom goes with physical beauty, but seldom fails to be impressive. This is no peasant parvenu, no Jean Balue, but a noble from the valley of the Loire, who had but given up the dignities of his own state to please the King whom he had served before the little Dauphin's death had given Orleans a throne, the King whose weakness he thoroughly understood and vigorously guided, and whose strength, which consisted in a genuine love for the people of France, D'Amboise knew equally well how to direct

CARDINAL D'AMBOISE
(drawn from the tomb in Rouen Cathedral, carved by Rouland Leroux).

into broad schemes of national security and unflinching administration of justice. If Louis' blunders in foreign politics could be redeemed at all, they were redeemed by the internal administration of his kingdom ; the evil counsels of the Italian Borgia or of his Breton wife were counterbalanced by the good order, the economy, and the reforms introduced by Cardinal d'Amboise into the French Government, which was sorely in need of help after the disorders of the last reign.

And if the Cardinal might fairly be reproached with an exaggerated ambition, a great longing for the highest place which the Church had to offer,[1] it was an ambition to which even stronger heads than his were to give way—the patriotism of Wolsey was no more free from the desire for the tiara than were the schemes of the French Cardinal, to whom the Englishman has so often been compared. No other man, say his contemporary critics, was so fitted for the papal throne as Cardinal d'Amboise; and the help of a countryman in so exalted a position would have been of no slight service to the King of France, who never saw his way clearly through the shifting kaleidoscope of European politics, and came utterly to grief after the Cardinal's death.

It is difficult to be severe in judging a king who stands almost alone in his affection for every class of his subjects. Torn in sunder by the disputes of the great barons of Charles VI.'s reign, harassed by the terrible English invasions, with no comprehension of the tortuous policy of Louis XI., and no sympathy with the scatterbrained chivalry of his son, the people of France welcomed with a universal

[1] There is a medal of this time with the head of the Cardinal on one side and on the other the papal tiara and keys, with the legend "tulit alter honores."

outburst of gratitude the rest and relief from taxation which this "Father of his Country" gave them, a rest which was only to be a brief breathing-space before the renewed restlessness, the extravagant expenditure of the reign of Francis I.

Nor was Louis XII. a King apart, a monarch unseen and unappreciated.[1] From his favourite home at Blois he had for long exercised a beneficent, if somewhat unthinking and indolent, influence over the central populations of the valley of the Loire. The young duke who appears in the high-shouldered fur cape with its long squared sleeves, in the round velvet cap that hides the lowness of the forehead and the heavy straight black hair of the portrait in the Gaignières collection, had grown into a stout, good-humoured, idle King, with full thick lips and heavy cheeks, a King with all the dreaminess of Charles d'Orléans and little of his originality, who could rule respectably and comfortably at home, but must fail hopelessly whenever the quick initiative of foreign expeditions was demanded of him.

The young gallants of the Court who had tasted of adventure in the campaigns of Charles VIII. could not rest quiet upon this side of the Alps: the results of Cæsar Borgia's embassy now became evident as well, and probably the schemes of Cardinal d'Amboise in connection with a possible election to the papacy would have been alone sufficient

[1] See the panegyric of his reign written by Claude Seyssel.

to induce the easy-going King to avenge his ill-fortune at Novara and make a fresh attack on Italy. The proceedings of Ludovico il Moro finally decided Louis. The story of the defeat and capture of Sforza has been already told.

This first campaign brought much importance to the Cardinal, who, as the representative of the King of France, and surrounded by the Marshal Trivulzio, the Bishop of Luçon, the Seigneur de Grammont, and many other notables, received in solemn state a deputation from the penitent Milanese, who "with four thousand little children, their heads bared, and clad in humble garments," as Jean d'Auton tells us, came in procession to entreat the favour of the Cardinal, who showed them by the mouth of one Michael Ris "leur déloyaute damnable, inexcusable trahison et irréparables défauts," and promised them their lives for the present and an examination of their requests for the future; after which the little children passing before him cried aloud, "France! France! miséricorde!"

A still more picturesque scene followed shortly afterwards at Pisa. For some time this unhappy town had enjoyed "a hazardous and agonised attempt at liberty," while Entragues and the French garrison which came in with Charles VIII.'s army refused to leave the citadel and abandon Pisa to Florence, her bitter enemy; and now the French envoys, who had been sent with difficult words of negotiation concerning the detested Florentine supremacy, were surrounded by "five or six hundred" young girls dressed in white, with two aged dames to lead them, and singing sweetly, 'devant l'image de Nôtre-Dame commencèrent les pucelles à chanter tant piteusement, et de voix si très lamentables que là n'y eut Français ni autre à qui du plus profond endroit du cœur jusqu'aux yeux ne montassent les chaudes larmes." With their tears and blandishments they so won the hearts of the rough soldiers that fighting became for the time impossible for mutual admiration ; the influence of women that was to exercise so great a power in France for the next century had begun, and had introduced one more disturbing element into the already confused system of Italian politics.

The next campaign was more disastrous for the arms of France, as was indeed only to be expected. The prodigies of valour performed by the Chevalier Bayard at the bridge of the Garigliano, and admiringly chronicled by the "Loyal Servitor," were not able to avert defeat from La Trémouille at the hands of the capable and politic General Gonsalvo di Cordova.

Between Cæsar Borgia and the Catholic King Ferdinand, France had been duped. The Spaniards had been let in by Naples, Cæsar Borgia had conquered the Romagna and taken in even Machiavelli, who was to give him immortality. The tragedies of the Vatican had but produced fresh complications for the French. Alexander VI. was carried a blackened swollen corpse, horribly dead by his own poisons, into St. Peter's, and Cæsar Borgia, almost unconscious and weakened at the very crisis of his fate by a mysteriously similar disorder, was chased out of Italy to die obscurely in a skirmish fighting for John d'Albret in Spain. The tiara had been very near to Georges d'Amboise, and there can unhappily be little doubt that it was his delaying of the French army, for interested motives, within reach of Rome, that hastened the disaster of Garigliano.

But a still greater blow to the true interests of France was only just averted at home. The misguided ambitions of Anne de Bretagne, dangerously strengthened by her Breton pluck and energy, had very nearly succeeded in giving to one man the crowns of France, Spain, Austria, and the Netherlands, in delivering up France to the power that was instinctively and most bitterly opposed to her. Her designs of marrying her daughter Claude to the child who was to become the Emperor Charles V. were most fortunately frustrated by the resolutions of the Estates of Tours.

But what little good had been effected by these was soon almost annulled by the blunders of the League of Cambrai. Venice was to be attacked, and Genoa to be humbled for her presumption in turning out the aristocratic party ; money was raised by the disgraceful method of selling the wretched Pisans to their cruel masters in Florence. So ill begun, this third Italian campaign was to continue with steadily-increasing ill-success. The new Pope, Julian de la Rovère, who had outwitted Cardinal d'Amboise and firmly established his power in the Vatican and the Romagna, soon turned round and joined Venice against France, and Louis XII. was still further weakened by the death of his old friend and steadfast counsellor, Georges d'Amboise.

Though the Cardinal died an immensely wealthy man, he had spent his riches lavishly, and made the best use of his opportunities for the encouragement of art with foreign models and Italian workmen ; but his loss as a statesman was far more severely felt. The good work he had begun in Normandy, "avec le titre effrayant de réformateur général," he had carried on throughout all the tribunals of France by means of his celebrated "ordonnances." In Italy, with the assistance of his brother Charles, Seigneur de Chaumont, he had invariably upheld the interests of France and guided the uncertain steps of the King through the maze of European politics with a hand that rarely faltered save when his one great fault became conspicuous, his too obvious ambition of the papal power. But it is on his home policy that his fame chiefly rests—his revision of justice, his measures for averting the famine while the so-called plague was devastating France, his swift repression of brigandage and violence.

His death, which was felt as a relief at the Vatican, was the signal for confusion in the mind of Louis. Austria and England were against him, the Pope had joined Ferdinand and Venice, and Louis felt the necessity of rousing himself to action. A new national infantry was formed by La Palice with a backbone of five thousand Gascons, and the young Gaston de Foix, the last of the house of Armagnac, the direct descendants of Clovis, at its head. The counsels of the veteran Marshal de Gié were lost to the King as well at this critical moment. Some years before he had been exiled by a disgraceful process, whose details only serve to throw into stronger light the honour and integrity of a life spent in loyal devotion to his country.

Besides all this, Louis was becoming more and more perplexed at the attitude of Margaret of Flanders. At all hazards, her father, Maximilian the Emperor, must be kept on the side of France, so at all hazards a victory must be won.

In the terrible day before Ravenna the French advanced between a double row of enemies, while the Spanish cannon "fired into the French infantry as into a great target, and killed more than two thousand of them before they came to blows." The Loyal Servitor and Bayard were fighting with the rest, and some sharp skirmishing followed between the cavalry of both sides; but it was the firm battalions of the newly-organised infantry that won the day for the French after fearful losses upon both sides. Bayard had warned the young Duc de Nemours to stay where he was after the battle had been decided, but Gaston saw some Spaniards making for Ravenna, and could not let them go unmolested. Riding out, directly his Gascons had told him of their passage, he attacked them furiously upon a narrow road with a canal on one side and a deep ditch on the other. He was almost alone with his cousin Lautrec, and was soon surrounded. When his charger was hamstrung, "he leaped down and sword in hand did braver deeds than ever did Roland at Roncevaux," and fell with all his wounds in front, and fourteen on his face. Bayard met the Spaniards at the other end of the road, some ten miles on, and not knowing of the death of the brave Gaston de Foix, let them pass safely on their way.

The tide of fortune had completely turned against the French, and round the same Novara which had seen so many crises of this unlucky war, La Trémouille was defeated and Italy was lost. But the quarrel over Milan, Naples, and Sicily was not yet fought out: Francis of Angoulême, the descendant of Valentine Visconti, claimed Milan because he was the heir to France by rights that were impregnable, until they were for ever lost at Pavia. The son of Francis, when he became Dauphin, missed one more chance of Milan, and the husband of Catherine de Medicis lost all hope of an Italian kingdom, which ended by being fast held by the Spaniards.

The crown of the two Sicilies, which was first held by the descendants of the Norman Robert Guiscard, had been claimed by the house of Hohenstaufen, and was in 1254 given by the Pope, who somewhat feared such strong neighbours, to the brother of Saint Louis, Charles d'Anjou. The quarrel that inevitably resulted was handed on through Louis XI., to whom René d'Anjou bequeathed his rights, to the Kings of France and even, through the house of Lorraine, to the Guises, who actually revived the old title, which had belonged to Anjou, of King of Jerusalem.[1] The new desire of national aggrandisement was joined to the fatal spirit of adventure, without losing the old religious ideal that had given nothing but a visionary basis to the policy of France, and uselessly wasted much French blood and treasure; the Sicilian Vespers were not redeemed by Marignano, and after the reign of Louis XII. the story of the French in Italy[2] closes in the defeat of Pavia and the excesses of the Constable Bourbon.

In 1513 died the Queen, Anne de Bretagne, at Blois. Fleurange and the Loyal Servitor describe the distress of Louis at the loss of her, but besides the

[1] Creighton's *Papacy*.

[2] "The story," that is, of the French in the period covered by these chapters, but it was not until the days of Napoleon that it was renewed.

King, and the poor whom she had assisted with her alms, there were not many to whom her death should have been a serious loss.[1]

Louis seemed more bewildered than ever in his attempts to distinguish the right path in the "danse Macabre" of European politics that followed. At last, amid the general quarrelling Henry VIII. of England gave Mary Tudor to be wife of the French King—a strong young Englishwoman, who killed off Louis within a year. There would be something ludicrous, if it were not pathetic, in the last months of this weak, easy-going King; he evidently was quite at a loss how to manage the young princess, and brought up his daughter Claude, Louise de Savoie, even old Anne de Beaujeu, to try and help him humour her.

"He had been used to dine at eight in the morning, now he dined at noon; his habit was to go to bed at six, and now he was often up till midnight," with the inevitable result of a serious illness which killed him by New Year's Day.

In 1559 Catherine de Medicis was at Chaumont. She had bought the property not so much for her

[1] In the Library of Corpus Christi College, Oxford, there is a memorial of Anne de Bretagne in the two volumes of an illustrated Bible presented by General Oglethorpe. The pictures were made for Louis XII., whose porcupine is conspicuous on the frontispiece, and for his Queen, whose cordelière is repeated on almost every page: it is probably the work of Jean Perréal, and should be compared with the same Queen's *Livre d'Heures*, part of which is in the Library of Tours, part in the Bibl. Nat.

own use as to provide herself with a suitable exchange for the more beautiful Chenonceaux, where her husband's favourite Diana had made herself so fair a home; and when the death of Henry II. brought Catherine into power, she turned Diana out and effected the desired exchange. But the Duchesse de Valentinois preferred Anet and the statue of Jean Goujon to Chaumont and the memories of Cardinal d'Amboise, so she too hardly visited the castle at all, and Chaumont for the next two centuries continually changed hands.

In 1739 Italy was again predominant, and the chimneys built by M. le Ray were smoking with the furnaces that baked the pottery and medallions of the Italian Nini. In 1803 Madame de Staël, in graceful exile, was chatting to Benjamin Constant on the long terrace above the river — the patron of Italian pottery had gone to lose his fortune on the other side of the Atlantic.

The firm tenure of its earlier proprietors seemed never destined to be repeated in the history of Chaumont, and the castle saw several more masters before coming into the possession of its present owner, the Duc de Broglie, by whom the old rooms are kept up in all the beauty and the interest of their earlier days.

Through the Salle des Gardes, all hung with tapestry, with its Italian fire-dogs of wrought iron, the visitor is led into the room of Diane de Poitiers, built in the thickness of the entrance tower. Her face looks down upon him from the wall, a calm, cold face beneath a crescent, that wears well, and will not be wrinkled or defaced by passion ; the three crescents and her monogram entwined with the royal H, show on the old tiling of the floor.

The great Salle de Conseil when we saw it was in a state of preparation for a "comédie, to be played by the Tsiganes from Paris," said the concièrge, and much of the fine oak carving with which the room was filled was hidden by the stage and its accessories ; but a more interesting apartment is farther on, the chamber of Catherine de Medicis, with its ancient bed and curtains, and its old worn prie-dieu beneath a curious group carved in one piece of oak.

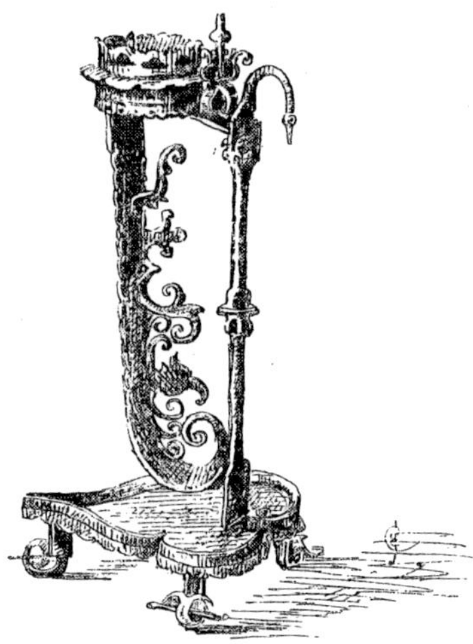

IRON CANDLESTICK (early fourteenth century) in the room used by Catherine de Medicis at Chaumont.

Here is to be seen the oldest tapestry of all, worked in soft colours of old rose and pink ; beside the door a blinded Love with rose-red wings and quiver walks on the flushing paths, surrounded by strange scrolls and mutilated fragments of old verses ; upon the wall in front are ladies with their squires attending, clad all in pink and playing mandolins, while by the stream that curves through flowery meadows small rosy children feed the water - birds that seem to blush with pleasure beneath the willow boughs of faded red. Much of the furniture of Chaumont does not possess the antiquity with which it has been associated, but these impossible landscapes with their quaint colouring and strange folk that people them may well have been here, with the old wrought-iron candlestick that stands before them, when Catherine de Medicis was wearing the extinguisher dress with its pink underskirt and deep fur sleeves in which she is portrayed in the next chamber, known as the "Chambre de Ruggieri." Upon the ceiling of this room are painted the dates when she and Cardinal d'Amboise were respectively at Chaumont, about a century apart, and in one corner the old weights stamped with the fleur-de-lys still suggest the reforms which D'Amboise carried out in the course of his strong government of France.

But a more especial memory of him is in the chapel, which is built in the form of a Greek cross with flamboyant windows. From the gallery that opens out into the west end from the upper stories of the house, we could see his old red Cardinal's hat still hanging above the carved chair in which he sat upon the altar steps ; there is a portrait of him too close by, so we were told, but we found it hard to recognise in this cavalier countenance with its moustache and imperial, and a very "roving eye," the stern lines of the Cardinal's rugged face upon his tomb at Rouen.

We descended to the courtyard again by the great staircase which sweeps in bold curving steps round the central pillar, and left the castle still thinking of "The Last Judgment" that hangs in the Chapel gallery. "The river of the wrath of God," and the countless souls caught up to heaven or dashed into the depths, seemed the true picture of the Italy of Georges d'Amboise, drawn by the real conscience of Italy herself, by him who alone had seized the spirit of the time, the mighty Michael Angelo.

FRANCIS I., AGED 34, from the enamelled terra-cotta bust in the possession of the Marquis de Bridieu, Château de Sansac, Loches.

*Reproduced by permission of M. Pericat, Tours.*

## CHAPTER XI

### REIGN OF FRANCIS I.

"Pharaoh, King of Egypt, is but a noise; he hath let the appointed time pass by."

"I promise you the effects he writes of succeed unhappily . . . death, dearth, dissolution of ancient amities, divisions in State, menaces and maledictions against King and nobles, needless diffidences, banishment of friends, dissipation of cohorts, nuptial breaches, and I know not what."

THE house of Valois provided heirs for the French throne for long after the direct line had died out; the line of Valois - Orléans had come in for a brief space and died without descendants, like its predecessors; that of Valois - Angoulême was now to appear, with whom the dynasty was to perish before the end of the century, blighted by the full measure of the remorseless curse which Italy had laid on France.

But this last line began with a splendour which

seemed to give but little presage of the ruin that was to come: there were probably few living besides the King himself who foresaw in the brilliant young Comte d'Angoulême[1] the man who was to undo all the good work of the previous reign and reap the full measure of its errors and his own.

At Amboise we shall meet the young duke growing between the evil angel and the good, his mother and his sister Margaret; there, too, beside the grave of the greatest of the Italians whom he favoured, we shall be able to appreciate his claims to praise as an art patron; but at none of the many châteaux of Touraine, where his influence is so conspicuous, can we catch a glimpse of Francis clear enough to serve as guide in judging of his character or of the value of his reign; not even at Chambord, that grotesque giant of the royal pleasure-houses, the Chambord which Brantôme saw even in his time but half-achieved, shall we find more than an indication of his reckless expenditure and unmeaning lavishness in the strange labyrinths of stone upon its roof, or a trace of the only lesson he could draw from the intrigues of a misspent existence in the cynical distich traced by his diamond ring upon the lost window-pane of his cabinet.

The delicate perfection of the staircase in the wing at Blois, by which the buildings of Louis XII.

[1] "Le grand garçon qui gâtera tout," as Louis called him.

were completed in the reign of Francis, remains to show that something better than Chambord was within the compass of French art, and possibly indicates that by the good taste of his wife Claude, who loved her old home in her father's favourite château, the strong and true instinct of the national school found more support than in the dilettante passion of Francis for the teaching of Florence and of Rome.

Yet so full is this Loire valley of the memory and the praise of Francis that we must stop for a while, before wandering farther along the river's banks, to take some measure of this prince's worth, and to look closer at his gentle, mystical sister, Marguerite d'Angoulême, Queen of Navarre. Upon their mother we have fortunately no need to dwell; in the most iniquitous trial of the reign, in the most horrible siege of that lawless generation, we shall see traces enough of the meanness of Louise de Savoie and the misgovernment of her despicable favourite the Chancellor Du Prat.

The character of Francis does not gain by a close inspection; and in this he is not unlike one of our own kings, Richard, son of the great Plantagenet, who figured as the perfect Paladin of ancient chivalry in many a poem and romance, who wasted English blood and treasure on visionary and useless expeditions, who only used his country, for the few months he ever spent in it, as a means of raising fresh supplies, and died at last fighting for an ignoble cause in an almost unknown corner of his French dominions.

It is much the same with this Amadis of a later Gaul, who took the Salamander for his device, but came out anything but unscathed from the furnace of his destiny. Perhaps no prince ever had so great an opportunity, and so lightly lost the chances of a time that was never to return. "Le grand garçon" of Amboise remained a childish adventurer, a mere stripling in intellect, to his life's end; the mature years which bring to graver men a power of judgment and a gift of true perspective brought little to Francis but an untimely weakening of bodily force, a fretful chafing at the reverses of his fortune. And this is obvious from a consideration of the way in which he met the two great influences with which his reign was brought in contact, the policy of the Emperor from without, the rising forces of the Reformation from within. "The Emperor tries in everything to do the very reverse of what I do," he complains to the Venetian ambassador Capello,[1] and a peevish sense of opposition, a small personal rivalry, is all that Francis saw in the famous struggle with Charles V. in which he failed, as he was bound to fail, in matching the puerile and unreasoning passion of a fantastic chivalry against the cold personification of an idea which made up the sombre character of Charles V. No greater

[1] *Rel. des Ambass. Venitiens,* Francesco Giustiniano, 1537.

contrast was ever presented upon contemporary thrones of Europe than the lives of these two princes, nor would it be fair to judge of the French King by a comparison with his rival, who represented the opposite extreme of thought and feeling.

The child of a woman who lost her reason, a sickly, epileptic youth,[1] Charles V. grew up to be one of the strongest, the most original figures in his time. Strange ideas of mysticism, of theocracy, mingle in this prematurely aged mind, and show themselves early in the subtlety and skill of the practised politician. Losing the penetrating influence that comes of human sympathy, he found nothing but the dogma of authority left to guide him in the rigid and indifferent system of a policy implacable as fate. Within three years Charles V. had conquered Montezuma in Mexico, and taken Francis prisoner at Pavia, yet against so redoubtable a foe the French King could only produce a fluctuating policy of ill-planned sieges and cartels of defiance. Accepting bravely, and with a full understanding, the position of opponent to the Emperor, Francis might have joined in one irresistible league the many forces antagonistic to the powers and aims of Spain and Austria, have secured the co-operation of England and the northern provinces of Germany, and offered a compact and invincible resistance to the scattered armies of the Empire ; but this he never realised,

[1] Coignet, *Fin de la vieille France* [*de Vieilleville*], cap. xix.

scarcely attempted. The Turks, who might have been left as a useful counterpoise to the eastern extremity of the Empire, and a standing menace to Vienna, were alternately summoned into the waters of the Mediterranean and menaced by the empty threat of a crusade; so, too, the Protestants, whose natural champion Francis was against the tyranny of Spain, were sometimes encouraged by alliances, sometimes burnt as heretics at the stake. The mistakes of Francis beyond the boundaries of his kingdom were not redeemed by any benefits conferred upon the populace within, and to the second of the two influences of his reign which were just mentioned Francis gives no more enlightened comprehension than to the first.

If Francis had encouraged the reform at all, it was only with the uncertain favour of a royal patron of research and letters; the sympathies of his sister with Calvin or with Marot had a deeper strain in them that was foreign to his nature. "Ne parlons point de celle-là, elle m'aime trop," he says to Montmorency, with a selfish satisfaction in her love for him that obscured any appreciation of the doctrines which she favoured.

Yet these doctrines of the Reformation were already deeply grafted in the soil of France. By the desolation of the civil wars, by the struggle of the Huguenot party against the forces of the nation, may be measured the depth and sincerity of the convictions from which those doctrines sprang ; and these civil wars were made possible by the political incapacity of Francis I., which, in spite of his occasional generous and lofty impulses, led him to precipitate the centralising movement of despotic monarchy. The same incapacity was renewed in Henry II., aggravated by a weakness of the Crown which permitted the formation of political parties. The Spanish marriage laid France open to the sombre and cruel fanaticism of Philip II., and the ruin was completed by the insatiable ambition, the astounding audacity of the Guises, favoured by the protection of their niece, Marie Stuart, on the throne of France ; the weakness, the irresolution, the lying spirit of Catherine de Medicis abandoned the nation first to one party and then to the other, and ended in never forming a national party at all.[1]

The reign of Francis opened characteristically with a magnificent expedition. "Madame," he writes to Louise de Savoie, who was left at home as Regent, "nous sommes dans le plus étrange pays où jamais fut homme de cette compagnie." One more expedition to Italy was starting with all the brilliancy of which the chivalry of France was capable. Upon the King's tomb in St. Denis the patient horses still tramp up the passes of the Alps, hauling the "grosse artillerie,"[2] while behind them wave the plumes of

[1] Coignet, *François I.*, p. xli.

[2] "Il nous fâche fort de porter le harnois parmi ces Montagnes . . .

the lansquenets and their long pikes leading the infantry, each man with a heavy arquebuse upon his shoulder.

Just before the battle the King was knighted by Bayard. "In truth," cries the good Chevalier, "you are the first prince whom ever I made knight; please God you never run away in battle." Marignano, at any rate, was a glorious victory, the first great fight the French had won since Agincourt. Bayard, and Pierre de Navarre with his "enfants perdus,"[1] and Lautrec were with the army; and Francis himself was fighting bravely with the rest, drinking the only water that could be got, all befouled with blood, when he was thirsty, and sleeping through the restless night upon a gun carriage.[2]

It had been better for Francis if this splendid victory, the last triumph of the feudal chivalry, had never been won; it was a dangerous precedent, that

croyez, Madame, que ce n'est pas sans peine; car si je ne fusse arrivé, notre grosse artillerie fût demeurée. Mais, Dieu merci, je la mêne avec moi."—*Lettres de François I.* Ap. Mignet, *Rivalité de François I. et de Charles V.*

[1] "Nos lansquenets en . . . trois troupes . . . la tièrce d'environ quatre mille hommes, que l'on appelle les enfants perdus de Pierre de Navarre."—*Letter of Francis I. to Louise de Savoie, 13th September* 1515, Michaud et Poujoulat, i. v.

[2] Fleurange "l'adventureux," who was knighted by the King after the battle, gives many details of the fighting. "Et demanda le dit seigneur (François) à boire, car il était fort altéré. Et y eut un piéton qui lui alla querir de l'eau qui était toute pleine de sang, qui fit tant de mal audit seigneur, avec le grand chaud, qu'il ne lui demeura rien dans le corps; et se mit dans une charette d'artillerie pour soi un peu se reposer et pour soulager son cheval qui était fort blessé."

led the unthinking King into the defeat of Pavia ; and the glitter of foreign successes was by no means reflected in prosperity at home, for Louise de Savoie and Du Prat were paramount in the affairs of State, and the Concordat had introduced a new system into ecclesiastical affairs, a system which was to result in the rise of the great political Churchmen, the favourites of kings who, by their own dissolute lives, were to condone the vices of their patrons. Yet one of the greatest of these same Churchmen might have been of service to Francis now, for he never learnt the lesson which it took a Richelieu to enforce, that France was stronger at home, and relying on her natural wealth and her unequalled situation, than she could ever be abroad.

And now the greatest of Francis' opportunities was to come and go. With all the prestige of his Italian campaign, with the borrowed lustre of his supposed protectorate of art and the Renaissance, Francis might well have posed as the champion of Europe against the encroaching powers of Spain and Austria, might well have carried the election against the silent and almost unknown Charles. But he was beaten in the election, and wasted the precious time afterwards in the useless pageant of the Field of the Cloth of Gold—a display in which Henry VIII. could perhaps better sympathise with the French King than any other reigning monarch would have done.

All the time his enemy was quietly plotting and combining, strengthening himself at home, even interviewing that same English King soon after the unprofitable festival in France had ended, and quietly coming to some kind of earnest understanding with him about the policy of Europe. And yet the first blow comes from Francis. To the north he sends out the Duc d'Alençon,[1] to the south Bonnivet, and Lautrec to Milan. The one chance that presented itself of crushing the Imperialists and even Charles himself was lost, and Lautrec was ignominiously beaten.

This last officer was received but coldly by the King on his return, for Francis was sore at the loss of the coveted duchy of Milan ; but Lautrec stoutly answered that the whole fault lay with his Majesty, who had been warned several times that without more money[2] Milan would be lost. The King in astonishment replied that four hundred thousand crowns had been despatched directly the request for them had reached him. Jacques de Beaune Semblançay, Superintendent of Finance, was forthwith summoned to explain matters, and announced

[1] Clement Marot celebrates this campaign in the verses beginning—

> " Devers Haynault sur les fins de Champaigne
> Est arrivé le bon duc d'Alençon,
> Avec honneur qui toujours l'accompaigne
> Comme le sien propre et vrai écusson," etc.

[2] The Swiss had deserted after the battle of Birocca, because their pay was not forthcoming. Lautrec felt able to speak boldly : he was the brother of the Comtesse de Châteaubriand.

that he had indeed received the money for despatch to Italy, but had handed it over to the King's mother, Louise de Savoie, upon her express command, and this he was prepared to prove.[1] He was thrown into prison by Louise, and for five years he was kept unjustly confined while her odious instrument Du Prat tried to heap up accusations against the most honourable man of his time, who under Charles VIII. and Louis XII. had held the same perilous office without a stain upon his character. The very warrant which at last condemned him, in August 1527, could not bring any precise accusations against the prisoner, but on a general charge of malversation decreed his death upon the gibbet of Montfaucon. For six hours he stayed by the scaffold waiting in vain for the royal pardon that never came, and at seven in the evening was hanged

[1] See Du Bellay's *Mémoires* (Martin du Bellay, xvii. 221). The scene is continued as follows :—"Le roi alla en la chambre de ladite dame avec visage courroucé, se plaignant du tort qu'elle lui avait fait d'être cause de la perte dudit duché ; chose qu'il n'eût jamais estimé d'elle, que d'avoir retenu ses deniers qui avaient été ordonnés pour le secours de son armée. Elle s'excusant dudit fait fut mandé ledit Seigneur de Semblançay, qui maintint son dire être vrai ; mais elle dit que c'étaient deniers que ledit S. lui avait de longtemps gardés, procédant de l'épargne qu'elle avait faite de son revenu ; et lui soutenait le contraire."

On questions of fact it is possible to take Martin du Bellay as an authority, though Montaigne warns us against believing his deductions, and being taken in by all his praise of François I. "Pour avoir l'entière connaissance," says the essayist, "du roi François et des choses advenues de son temps, qu'on s'addresse ailleurs, si on m'en croit." Even in this episode we have to seek elsewhere for the details of the disgraceful condemnation in which this trial ended.

amid the indignation of the whole of France.[1] The death of this just man is one of the blackest stains upon the reign of Francis. He should never have allowed the meanness and cupidity of his mother to have such terrible results:[2] but an even worse instance of the evil which this despicable woman could bring to pass was soon to be seen in the extraordinary episode of the Constable Bourbon.

Anne, who was Regent in the first years of Charles VIII., had by her husband, Pierre de Bourbon, a child, Suzanne, who had been at first betrothed to the Duc d'Alençon; but feeling a greater attraction towards the young Charles, Duc de Montpensier,

[1] Clement Marot's verses express the feeling of the time—

"Lorsque Maillard, juge d'enfer, menait
À Montfaucon Semblançay l'âme rendre,
À votre avis lequel des deux tenait
Meilleur maintien? pour vous le faire entendre,
Maillard semblait homme que mort va prendre,
Et Semblançay fut si ferme vieillard
Que l'on cuidait pour vrai qu'il menât pendre
À Montfaucon le lieutenant Maillard."

One of Semblançay's houses was at Ballan, near Tours.

[2] There is practically no doubt that Louise de Savoie obtained this money upon false pretences, stole or made away with the receipts, and sacrificed Semblançay to avoid discovery, for avarice was among her many sins. She died with fifteen hundred thousand gold crowns in her money chests. Gaillard (*Hist. de François I.*, 1769) quotes two letters, one from Semblançay, the other of her own, which conclusively prove these facts. In Sauval (*Antiquités de Paris*, i. 482) are reported the details of the execution at Montfaucon, quoted from a manuscript journal, and Du Bouchet (*Annales d'Aquitaine*) describes the long wait by the gibbet, and the last words of the old man when he found himself abandoned by the King. Even Brantôme cannot gloss over the iniquity of the proceedings, though he shifts the blame as much as possible from Francis to his mother.

a younger son of the great house of Bourbon, she married her daughter to him in spite of the opposition of the King. Georges d'Amboise performed the ceremony of betrothal. Michelet has pointed out the mistake made by a daughter of Louis XI. in thus concentrating in the bold and reckless person of the young duke such vast feudal possessions.[1] A few years after his marriage we find the duke with Louis XII. before Genoa, and with an important command at Milan ; later on he is with young Gaston de Foix at Ravenna, and is made Constable of France by Francis. At Marignano he is in the vanguard of the army, which had already owed so much to his care and guidance in the passes of the Alps, and in 1517 the King himself assists at the magnificent baptismal fêtes of the duke's son and heir at Montlieu. But Bourbon had already reached the summit of his fortunes, and a change was at hand. The covetousness and rancour of Louise de Savoie had already led her to detest the greatness of the Constable and the virtue of his wife, and for some time she had been striving to prejudice the King against them. In 1521 the first blow was struck, the first insult given, the command of the vanguard was transferred to the Duc

[1] See Du Bellay's *Mémoires*, and Marillac, *Vie du Connétable.* The Constable united in himself the various dignities of Bourbon, Auvergne, Montpensier, Foix, and La Marche ; in the south, Carlat, Murat, and Annonay ; in the east, Beaujolais and Dombes ; besides the possessions in Poitou and Picardy, which he held as the descendant of St. Louis, and the emoluments resulting from his public offices.

d'Alençon. Misfortunes followed thick and fast. All his three children died, and were followed by their mother to the tomb. This was the moment for Louise de Savoie to appear. She immediately laid claim to all the lands of the Constable that had come to him through Suzanne de Bourbon, as being the nearer relation of the two ; and an even more odious motive for her hatred soon became apparent. Reckless in her desires as she was unprincipled in action, Louise had conceived for the Constable a passion which was repulsed with all the aversion and disdain it merited. This added the most poignant motive to her spite. By the machinations of her creatures, Du Prat, Poyet, and the Advocate-General Lizet, she at length drove the Constable in sheer despair into treason and exile. Some of his accomplices we have already met with in the dungeons of Loches. Bourbon himself, his plots against the throne discovered, fled out of France,[1] and threw himself under the protection of the Emperor, who was but too glad to receive so welcome an ally. The sequel is worthy of so terrible a beginning, and the tragedy of his life ended in the sack of Rome.

After two such disasters within his kingdom the fortunes of Francis fared no better abroad. In the spring of 1525 a letter was brought to Louise de Savoie from Pizzighitone. "Madame," wrote the King, "pour vous faire savoir comme se

[1] The details of the flight are given in Du Bellay's *Mémoires*.

porte le reste de mon infortune, de toutes choses ne m'est demeuré que l'honneur[1] et la vie qui est sauve." Pavia had been lost, the King had barely escaped with life, and the little honour he had left was to be cast aside in the bitter trial of his captivity. It was in great part his own want of generalship which had lost the battle—he made an attack in front of his own guns "tellement qu'il couvrit son artillerie et lui ôta le moyen de jouer son jeu" (Du Bellay). Cut off by the enemy completely, he had his horse killed under him, and was borne to the ground and taken prisoner; Bonnivet and old Louis de la Trémouille were killed fighting by his side;[2] Chabannes fell with the vanguard; the Maréchal de Foix, the Bastard of Savoy, and many more were captured by the enemy. After some delay the King was moved to Madrid and kept a close prisoner in the castle.

France was now deprived not only of the head of her Government, but of many of her best counsellors and fighting men. Bayard had been wounded to the death in the retreat from Biagrasso, and the Loyal Servitor had watched his burial in the Monastère des Minimes, near Grenoble.

The good Queen Claude had died, too, at her

[1] The origin of the famous "Tout est perdu fors l'honneur."

[2] Du Bellay describes the battle, and Sébastien Moreau gives more details about the part which the outlawed Duke of Suffolk and the exiled Constable took in the fighting. For portraits of La Trémouille and De la Palisse (Chabannes), see *Bibl. Nat. Estampes*, Q. b. 18.

château of Blois, leaving her three sons and two daughters to the care of Marguerite, the loving sister of the King, whose husband, D'Alençon, died of shame at his disgrace at Pavia. And now Francis began to fret himself into a mortal sickness behind his prison bars. All Europe began to feel some sympathy for his misfortunes—the sympathy of the Spanish ladies soon grew into a warmer feeling; but the captive King grew worse and worse, and the cold Emperor remained relentless. In alarm at what might happen, Marguerite set out for Spain. The keynote of her character is this passionate love for Francis, which acknowledged no fault, recognised no failing in her ideal hero. As she travels slowly southwards, when there is no one by to watch her tears, she consoles herself with writing down her gentle words of grief; the litter moves too slowly for her fears—

> "Une heure me dure cent ans
> Et me semble que ma litière
> Ne bouge ou retourne en arrière,
> Tant j'ai de m'avancer désir."

So, later on, will this patient "Madame Oiselle" write her *Heptameron*, as the litter swings through the pleasant roads of France while Brantôme's grandmother sits by, to amuse her brother in his last failing months of life. But at this time deliverance did not come from her, though she brought the King encouragement and health. Her letters to him after she had left Madrid to try and negotiate for his release [1] touchingly show how soon her hopes of success were to be disappointed. The Emperor was not a man to be influenced by her personality, or agree with her requests.[2] A useless proposal for abdication was all she could bring back to France.

MARGUERITE D'ANGOULÊME, QUEEN OF NAVARRE, sister of Francis I.

After this, for a time, she is not prominent in

[1] See Lanz, *Correspondance de Charles V.*, p. 179. An account of her first interview with the Emperor at Toledo was read to the Parliament in Paris at the sitting of 19th October 1525. "Il me tint fort bons et honnêtes propos," she writes to Francis.

[2] Babou writes to Montmorency on 5th October of the second interview: "Là nous ont été tenus les plus hautes termes jusqu'aux menaces. Il leur a été répondu doucement." And Marguerite tells the King, "Je voyais bien qu'ils étaient empêchés de moi, me voulant rendre contente sans rien vouloir faire de la raison." And above: "Il y avait en eux peu d'honneur ou beaucoup de mauvais vouloir."

politics. She married Henry, King of Navarre, who had escaped from his guards after Pavia, and had a daughter, the famous Jeanne d'Albret, who was to marry Antoine de Bourbon and be the mother of Henry IV., le bon Béarnais, the witty husband of another Marguerite far different from this first one.

So in her quiet cultured Court at Nérac Marguerite of Navarre lives for these next years apart, laughing over the jests of Rabelais, talking with the Du Bellays of the Collège de France, thinking often over the more serious subjects of which she had written to her good friend the Bishop of Meaux during the first distresses of the war, and giving a refuge to Calvin and a helping hand to Estienne, busy over his Latin Bible.

At last the impatient royal prisoner was released, and galloped across the frontier to Bayonne, leaving his children in his stead as pledge for the extravagant promises which he had only made to break.

The country was sadly in need of guiding and of government, but Francis' first thought is to escape the serious tasks of business and the toil of State affairs, and to compensate himself for the imprisonment that had already undermined his strength, by fresh luxury and excitement among the ladies of his Court. One of the results of the negotiations for his release had been his engagement to Eleanor, sister of the Emperor, a woman of a pronouncedly German type, of great kindness and little wit, with a dash of the romantic in her character that had shown itself in an early attachment to the Prince Palatine Frederic, her companion at the Court of Lorraine. Her features were strongly marked, and she had the true Austrian lip; for the rest, a pink and white face with black curved brows and smiling eyes.[1]

But this was not enough to content the roving Francis, in a Court where, as Brantôme tells us, "toute la décoration venait des dames." His first mistress was Françoise de Châteaubriand, of the famous house of Foix, but at Bayonne he remembered that it was quite ten years since she had first attracted him, and looking among his mother's maids of honour for some newer flame to stimulate his jaded senses, he lighted on the young Anne de Pisseleu. To see was to conquer, and Brantôme relates how he put off the old love and took on the new, apparently quite forgetting his betrothed Eleanor in the whole transaction.

Meanwhile very different scenes were going on in the unhappy towns of Italy. Bourbon had come back at the head of the imperial troops, joined by the ruffians who had been attached to Frundsberg. Don Pedro's men were in the north, the "bandes noires" of Jean de Médicis in the south, the Lorrainers in Naples, and town after town was

[1] *Vie du Palatin Frédéric*, Thomas de Liège.

ravaged and destroyed by freebooters, who had already swept the country, and left but little for the starving peasants.

With such a state of things in Italy, and such a man as Bourbon ready to dare anything in a despairing bid for fortune, a catastrophe was inevitable. He offered himself as the leader of this cut-throat rabble, and they received him with enthusiasm.[1]

A standard-bearer on the walls of Rome,[2] early in May 1527, suddenly saw some of Bourbon's soldiers and their chief himself advancing through the vines. His consternation betrayed a weak place in the defence. In a moment the whole of this infernal company are in motion pouring down upon the Eternal City from the hills behind the Vatican like vultures upon their prey. At the first alarm Benvenuto Cellini had caught up a musket like the rest, and running to the ramparts had the address, as he tells us himself, to pick off the leader with a shot in the groin.[3] The reckless exile was dead, and amid scenes which were a fitting ending to the last terrible months of his existence. The desperadoes behind him poured into

[1] One of their drinking songs ended—

> "Calla, calla, Julio Cesar, Annibal y Scipion,
> Viva la fama de Bourbon!"

[2] He was guarding "la muraille du bourg Saint Pierre."—Du Bellay.

[3] See *Life of Benvenuto Cellini*, by J. A. Symonds, vol. i. p. 91, and note.

Rome unchecked, and the most ghastly horrors of a siege began, that spared neither age nor sex, and desecrated sacred and profane alike. Where Goths and Vandals of an earlier age had feared to tread, these ruffians, the offscouring of the most brutal mercenary corps in Europe, burnt, pillaged, massacred, and gorged themselves with plunder until the plague broke out in the desolated city, and the soldiers had to fly for safety to the open country from the streets choked with the most hideous forms of death.[1]

At the same time there was terrible distress throughout France, for the heavily-taxed peasantry were shivering and half-starved in the provinces, while their "theatrical prince" was spending thousands on a thriftless Court. There is a great change in Francis on his return from Madrid. A beaten King, a King who publicly repudiates his promised word, can no longer pose as the champion of European chivalry; and even within his kingdom his prestige was waning. Lautrec was dead, Charles was once and for all established in Italy and acknowledged as the most powerful prince in Europe, and in France the Reformation had already split up the Court into parties whose formation the King felt himself too weak to crush.

[1] Du Bellay gives a short account of the taking of Rome; but a terribly realistic picture of the scenes that followed will be found in the *Sack of Rome*, by Jacques Bonaparte (first part in Italian, at Cologne, 1756).

In September 1531 a welcome and unexpected sum of money came into the King's treasury. His mother, Louise de Savoie, died, leaving enough treasure for the King to complete the payment of his ransom and to begin the equipment of another army. He had probably never realised the extent of this woman's avarice and wickedness. The firmness and courage which she could occasionally show obscured faults to which even a son should not have been blind ; and, if in nothing else, in her patronage of Du Prat was displayed the recklessness with which she could make use of the vilest instruments in the attainment of her ends.[1]

Just a year before, Francis had made a real step in the right direction by beginning a sound political combination against Charles V. He had several sympathies with the English King Henry, and they could agree at least in a common mistrust and

[1] She must have known the universal detestation in which her favourite was held. In the streets of Lyons people sang—

"Ort Chancellier, Dieu te maudye,
Desloyal traitre conseiller ;
Par toy le Roy est prisonnier
Dont tu perdras en bref la vye,
Ort Chancellier.

. . . . .

Tu feiz au Roy chasser Bourbon
Duquel le conseil estoit bon ;
Il nuisoit à ta mengerye,
Ort Chancellier."

He had done so much evil that at last every misfortune was ascribed to him indiscriminately.

dislike of the crafty character of the Emperor, so different from their own.

The mutual promises of the Field of the Cloth of Gold were renewed upon a firmer basis, in an interview near the same place twelve years later, and the Protestant princes who had just formed the League of Smalkald were quite prepared to join the two princes against Charles. But Francis, blind as ever to the true issues of a consistent policy, and always prone to let his passion for Italy prove a besetting snare, betrothed his second son to Catherine, the last of the house of the famous Cosmo de Medicis. It was an utterly disproportionate match, that appealed to the pride of Clement VII. without in the least affecting the position of the French in Italy, for the Pope died in the next year; it was of serious harm to the Protestant alliance, and even caused the grave annoyance of the English King, whose part in the bargain was never accomplished to his mind; its consequences in the future were still more fatal, for it introduced into the heart of France the poisonous influence of a woman who was to become its Queen and to continue her fatal plots and machinations until the end of the century.

Meanwhile the power of Charles was growing fast. As the conqueror of Barbarossa he was almost the champion of Christendom, while he could point to France as the ally of Soliman and the heretics. His contempt at last openly broke out in the extraordinary speech, which Du Bellay has reported, before the Pope in the Consistory. His attack upon the south of France was only warded off by the brutal methods of Montmorency, who laid waste the whole of Provence to compel the Imperialists to retire for lack of food.

The Protestants were growing desperate of help. Already Geneva, in 1536, began to be troubled with insurrections, and the Eidgenossen of the Huguenots were forming with the watchwords of their teacher Calvin. The King himself had openly given up all pretence of championing their cause, and joined the Spanish party of Montmorency and the Dauphin. A strange result of this changed policy was the visit of the Emperor to France—we shall hear of him at Amboise and elsewhere—but it ended in nothing better than the disgrace of the Constable when the futility of all attempts at reconciliation became evident after Charles had returned.

A third war began, in which the only profits were won by the Turks, who sailed with their booty to Constantinople. Cerissoles and the victories of Montluc were barren of results except for the rise in importance of the Guises, who were to play so large a part in the next half-century. The reign of Francis was drawing to its close. In 1545 died Luther, and in 1547 the English King, in whose death Francis saw a warning of his own; both he and the Emperor were growing old before their time, but the French King was to go before his rival ; and Francis was one of those men who can ill afford to grow old. The gaiety of his youthful temperament was turned to a morose irritability, the bloom of his first beauty was changed by the disfigurements of disease. Amid the quarrels of his mistresses, the disputes of his old friends, with all his grief for the death of his eldest son, and his annoyance at the attitude of the Dauphin, who between his Italian wife and the cold counsels of Diane de Poitiers seemed completely estranged from the sympathy of his father, Francis feverishly wore out the last days of his existence : some solace, some consolation, indeed, was given him by the presence of his sister Marguerite, who tries tenderly to amuse him at Chambord with her conversation, to write him stories in her *Heptameron* ; but he cannot rest. He hurries through Touraine from one hunting seat to another, striving to forget his pain of body and distress of mind in violent exercise, but must needs stop at last for very agony at Rambouillet, and there die.

In spite of all his faults and failures Francis has always exercised a strange fascination over his countrymen. "If he was not a great King," writes one, "he was at any rate a great man." "Regulus, it is true, was more virtuous," says another ; "let men like Regulus condemn him." Brantôme and Du Bellay are full of his praises, and they have been echoed by their compatriots ever since. And perhaps this is because he is so distinctively a type of one side of the French character. "François, ici présent, qui est tout Français," as Thomas Birco calls him at the Estates of Tours which confirmed his marriage with the daughter of Louis XII.: something, too, of the lustre of the changeful times he lived in has fallen upon him, and lent to the King the fame of a Renaissance that came but from the progress of the ages.

In the reign of Francis the effect of many great discoveries first began to be felt. The discovery of America had created a revolution in commerce, had cheapened the precious metals, had created capitalists; the route round the Cape of Good Hope had enlarged the boundaries of trade; the wars across the Alps had led men's minds to Italy, that old enchantress with "the fatal gift of beauty" even in the years of her decay, and with an added interest from the stores of classical research just opened to the world of scholarship and thought. Italy was the soil of heroes, where the chivalry of a later day was to try its maiden steel amid the new and changing scenes of European politics, where Bayard met in fight the sons of Cortes and Pizarro, who had seen the fall of Mexico and Peru, where Michael Angelo was striving, alone and unassisted, to show an unheeding generation the warnings of this world and the next.

Among all this comes the great change, the mighty movement of the Reformation, the beginning of modern times ; a movement which awakened old notions of equality, for it began among the poor and ignorant, which changed a military society into one civil and industrial, which, like Socrates, brought ideas into the world and taught the liberty of philosophical opinion in the face of an irresistible political despotism.

And it is with this intellectual part of the movement of reform that Marguerite of Navarre is especially associated, though she had been obliged to hide her sympathies from her brother ; and now that he was dead the light seemed to have gone out of her life. Her oldest friends had left her or were dead, and in her contemplative seclusion at Nérac she quietly and sadly lived her last years, conversing with Montluc, Bishop of Valence, with Lefebvre d'Être, librarian of Blois, writing to Amyot, the professor of the university at Bourges, or exchanging graceful fancies with her poet Marot. "Hers was a mind," says Michelet, "delicate, swift, subtle, which fluttered over everything, lighted on everything, and scarcely went beneath the surface." And Rabelais, too, with a keen appreciation of her character, writes in his dedication—

> "Esprit abstrait ravy et ecstatic,
> Qui frequentait les cieux son origine."

And her love for Francis is the sun she follows, "non inferiora secutus." This pale princess is his good genius among the evil influences of a Court of favourites where there was none like Agnes Sorel ; when he deserted her, he left his fortune with her. " Earth had conquered heaven."

The quaint stories she has left in literature, with the delightful interludes of conversation that are their chief charm, have all the indecency but little of the immorality of their time. To fully grasp what that immorality was we have but to look at the extraordinary Memoirs of Cellini, the type of the strange age in which he lived, who seems to have lost all discrimination between wrong and right, to be devoid of any moral sense, wholly given up to the physical pleasures of a life as full as he could make it, or to the keen passion for the beautiful in art, of which he was so great a master. One more thing, that is but another reflection of the temper of the times, is very noticeable in this autobiography : there is a great contempt for human life, a hideous familiarity with death that shows itself again and again in what that century has left for us to see and pity. The woodcuts of Hans-Sebald Beham are full of the " faucheurs de la mort," the terrible skeletons in tatters that follow hard upon the plundering lansquenets. At Lyons men were studying Holbein's " simulachres de la mort," those wild imaginations of ever-present death, where the grinning skull shows close behind the Pope's tiara, where a skeleton upon the battlefield smites down the soldier with a human bone, or in the doctor's study take the fees from his last patient, or with the ghastly music of his bagpipes lures on the maniac to destruction.

> . . . "Comme sur un drap noir,
> Sur la tristesse immense et sombre
> Le blanc squelette se fait voir . . .
> . . . Des cercueils lève le couvercle
> Avec ses bras aux os pointus,
> Dessine ses côtes en cercle
> Et rit de son large rictus."

There is a fragment in the Museum of Namur, a mailed knight to the waist without a head, holding in its hands a skull; beneath is the inscription, "Une heure viendra quy tout paiera," and the letters N and P joined by a true lovers' knot. It is a fragment that shows pathetically the terror, the injustice, the wild dreams of vengeance of those times, when no man's life or woman's virtue was safe, when the inevitable sadness of the grave was redoubled by strange shapes of death personified and hideously exultant.

In this sombre picture the form of Marguerite stands apart, a light that was soon to fade. Her death at the Castle of Odos in December 1549 was one more triumph for the party that had always been in opposition to her and to her instincts. The sun had set, and "the pale crescent of Diana" began its slow and sure ascent, chilling with its cold beams the reign of Henry II.

Diane de Poitiers, Duchesse de Valentinois, is enthroned at Chenonceaux.

# CHAPTER XII

## CHENONCEAUX

"Lors se bastissoyt aux soings de Messire Bohier, général des finances, le chasteau de Chenonceaulx, lequel, par mignardise et curiosité boutoyt son bastiment à cheval sur la rivière du Cher."

"There is a sore evil which I have seen under the sun, namely, riches kept for the owners thereof to their hurt. But those riches perish by evil travail: and he begetteth a son and there is nothing in his hand."

AMONG the first acts of the new King after the death of Francis I. was the gift of the royal domain of Chenonceaux to Diane de Poitiers, with whose name the château has ever since been associated. But, though it is in the Italian gardens of Diana that the story of Chenonceaux touches its highest point of interest, this, the most lovely of the "plus excellents bastiments de France," has seen a long line of châtelaines.

Ladies ruled there even before Diana, and the last have but lately left this home among the naiads of the Cher, which seemed especially dedicated to the grace and luxury of women.

Some distance eastward of the bridge of Tours, between the rivers of the Loire and Indre, nestles the little village of Chenonceaux, in the shade of the great forest of Amboise. The railway, which soon leaves the valley of the Loire, had entered the vale of the Cher, and passed the main drive of the château before we had realised the situation ; and in a few moments an omnibus, drawn at an astonishing pace by one of those French horses of the Percheron breed which never seem to tire and are rarely out of condition, brought us to the inn of the Bon Laboureur in the village, where a primitive but extremely well-cooked déjeuner awaited us.

We had caught a glimpse of the roof of the château, broken by its countless points and gables, as we drove up, and as soon as the bottle of Vin Mousseux was finished and appreciated we were fairly on our way to explore more closely the home of so many beauties famous in French history.

The fine drive to the doors is guarded by two stone sphinxes, and, though the railway crosses it, it is at a distance which obviates any annoyance from the sleepy and infrequent trains.

The first view of Chenonceaux is a magnificent

one. On the immediate right is the long range of splendid stables—a modern building, but of good taste; and to the left spreads the wide terraced garden built by Diane de Poitiers, surrounded by its high walk which leads to the raised courtyard immediately in front of the main building, a large and very handsome open space rising upon high walls from the lower level, with a fine detached tower at the right corner, the oldest part of the château, the last relic of its earliest owners. It bears the initials of Thomas Bohier and Catherine Briçonnet his wife, upon the beautifully carved doorway at its base, and is crowned by a huge extinguisher of slate, while the lines of its sides are gracefully relieved by a smaller turret clinging to its walls, whose pointed top breaks the outline of the larger roof. Immediately to the left of this is the great drawbridge leading to a strong circular stone pier rising out of the waters of the Cher; then begins the main building of the château, that fairy-like construction which owed its birth to Catherine Briçonnet.

In early times a Roman villa seems to have stood upon this site, too lovely to be left long without an occupant. The vine-lands slope down softly to the river's edge, and the trees and foliage round the water help to make an exquisite natural setting for one of the most beautiful dwellings ever fashioned by the art of man. Later on the site was filled by a rough kind of feudal castle, to which, in

VIEW OF CHENONCEAUX FROM THE ENTRANCE DRIVE, showing the terraced gardens of Diane de Poitiers on the left.

the time of the Marques (between 1250 and 1500), a watermill had been added.

Jean Marques had sided with the English against the son of Charles VI., and by his traitorous adherence to the invaders caused so much annoyance that the town of Tours summoned Du Guesclin to come to the assistance of the province. Close by the castle he defeated the English, razed the fortifications of the place, and cut down its woods "à l'hauteur de l'infamie," as a punishment for the unpatriotic behaviour of their owner. In 1432 a second Jean got letters-patent from Charles VII. for raising the outworks again, and rebuilding the donjon, and in the next year the moats were dug and the corner tower built. Jean died in 1460, heavily in debt, and Pierre, with an equal disregard of the first principles of finance, bought land and built on it until the family was ruined and the estate heavily mortgaged.

Such was the state of Chenonceaux when Catherine Briçonnet came to transform it. The feudal castles were gradually decaying, and the power of the Bourgeois that rose with the rising of the Renaissance was represented by her husband, Thomas Bohier. The main buildings of the older pile she entirely demolished, except the one tower which still stands in the corner of the raised courtyard before the main door of the château. The building—call it villa, castle, château, what you will—was at any rate no longer to be a fortress, and indeed there had never been much serious fighting (if we except the operations under Bertrand du Guesclin long before) round a home which was destined for all its future to be almost the only great château in France without the stain of murder on its walls.

In the improvements which this first Catherine initiated, the old piles and massive masonry of the mill were cleverly made use of, and upon this solid base, made somewhat larger, the main body of Chenonceaux was built with a taste so exquisite and so original that the uncertainty which hides the name of the architect is doubly to be deplored. Mrs. Mark Pattison, whose notes on the architecture of Touraine gracefully supply so much that is wanting in the more serious treatises of Viollet le Duc or Petit, considers that the plans of Chenonceaux may be ascribed to the same Pierre le Nepveu dit Trinqueau who is responsible later on for the gigantic courts of Chambord: if so, the earlier building gains immensely from the greater restraint and refinement of the artist's handling, while it loses nothing of that wild spirit of invention which is the characteristic of a transitional period in which men feel their way towards constructive change, "not daring to touch essential features, but tentatively busy on the transformations and adaptations of minor details."

The Renaissance had a far earlier origin in France than is usually given to it; the definite fixing of any limits to a period of change is always dangerous, often impossible. By the time the English had been expelled the old defensive architecture was known to be practically useless, and the transition, which is especially noticeable at Loches, had already begun. In the same line of building the narrow openings for arrow-shots and the unbroken line of thick protecting wall had given place to rooms that opened to the light, with windows carved and arabesqued. What was needed was not the foreign arts of Primaticcio,[1] but a firm national government at home, which was ensured by peace and signalised by the rise of the master masons and the builders of the great cathedrals.

There were many pilgrimages to the Holy Sepulchre before the first Crusade, and so it was because the fifteenth century dreamed of Italy that the sixteenth went there, and found instead of free development the bondage that ensued from fuller knowledge. But of this first pure dream, this earlier time of reawakening and national strength [2] unfettered by Italian schools, Azay-le-Rideau and Chenonceaux remain among the most perfect examples.

"Tourelles break out from the massive walls at points where they cease to suggest the flanking

[1] See the article on Chenonceaux, by M. James Darmesteter, *Revue Bleue*.

[2] See Chap. VI. on the House of Orleans, the earlier pages on the art of Touraine.

towers which they originally replaced. Every turret, every pinnacle, is crowned with some fantastic ornament, and the angles at which gables jut forth here and there from the pierced and carved work which surrounds them, are selected with the express intention of misleading the eye ; but the heavy cones which surmount the larger towers thrust through the ornaments which flame about them, and bring a sense of order into troubled places, even where every element of design seems absent." [1]

Nor is the interior less remarkable with halls and corridors and antechambers multiplying mysteriously. The contrast between the rooms of Langeais and of Chaumont becomes a still greater one here ; the few high halls that sufficed for Jean Bourré at Langeais would never have satisfied the enlarged ideas of a life apart as well as a life in common, for which the architect of Chenonceaux was bidden to provide.

With many of Thomas Bohier's relations we have already become acquainted. He was, for instance, a connection of the Chancellor Du Prat, a son-in-law of Cardinal Briçonnet, a nephew of Jacques de Beaune Semblançay, and he held the post of General of the Finances in Normandy ; he was one of the great financiers who were in many ways the precursors of

[1] Mrs. Mark Pattison, *Renaissance of Art in France*, cap. ii. Chenonceaux was complete (all save the bridge across the Cher) by 1517. The wing of Francis I. at Blois was being built in 1515, Chambord and Azay about 1526, Fontainebleau in the next year.

the famous and unhappy Fouquet, but as our sympathies are often more in favour of the magnificent good taste of the minister of Louis XIV. than against the recklessness of his expenditure, so if these earlier "surintendants" greatly sinned they left the beauty of their châteaux as an enduring excuse for their shortcomings.

For some time Semblançay had been buying lands for Bohier all round the embarrassed estates of the Marques family, who, after much struggling to keep their old home, were finally bought out in 1499 with certain legal restrictions and feudal complications still unsettled. For seven years more Bohier continued to buy up land in all directions, until at last he was able to become the sole possessor of Chenonceaux, bidding against the "grand maître des arbalétriers de France." But the Crown had something to say in the acquisition of this coveted estate, and Bohier, after spending 26,812 livres on the place, was made to pay further sums as compensation for taking up certain royal privileges; but more and more land on all sides was bought up, and the reconstruction of the château was begun, of which Bohier himself was never to see the completion. His position at this time gave him immense power and control over the revenues of the kingdom, and his proud motto, "S'il vient à point me souviendra," seemed almost justified, when in 1521 he went with Lautrec as Treasurer-General on the

Italian expedition. In the affair of the loss of the King's money already explained, Bohier paid the soldiers out of his own pocket, and was made Lieutenant-General. He died in 1524, at Vigelli, in the same retreat in which Bayard perished, and his uncle Semblançay, at the age of eighty-two, was hanged at Montfaucon to save the tarnished honour of Louise de Savoie.

The magnificent preparations of Chenonceaux had a sad ending enough. Perhaps it would have been possible for a scion of a royal house only, or an official in such high position as that of Thomas Bohier, to have done what he did for his château; but whether his immense wealth was all got honestly or not, he seems to have left but little comfort behind him, for Catherine Briçonnet died but two years afterwards, and his son's days were early embittered by the harassing task of trying to square the confused accounts of his father. The rest of Antoine's life was made up of financial quibbles and questionable arrangements, which throw a strange light on the business honesty of the times, and explain much of the after history of Chenonceaux.[1]

[1] De Tocqueville explains very forcibly the distressing position of these "Surintendants de Finance," who from Marigny to Necker were between the devil and the deep sea. "La produit des taxes si mal reparties avait des limites, et les besoins des princes n'en avaient plus. Cependant ils ne voulaient ni convoquer les états pour en obtenir les subsides, ni provoquer la noblesse en l'imposant à réclamer la convocation de ces assemblées. De là vient cette prodigieuse et malfaisante fécondité de l'esprit financier durant les trois derniers siècles de la

The heir of Thomas Bohier's complicated balance-sheets was given all his father's offices as well, with the unpleasant result that in 1531 he was declared a debtor for an enormous sum to the Treasury. Antoine at once made arrangements with his brothers to amalgamate their common property, and, by adding Chenonceaux itself to the money he was thus enabled to raise, he found it possible to satisfy the demands of Anne de Montmorency, the creditor for the Crown. He was forgiven the rest by Francis I., "en bonne foi et parole de roi," and for the present seemed quit of the whole unpleasant business. Chenonceaux had become a Crown domain, and a series of royal visits soon began.

Now Francis often came over from his Court at Plessis-lez-Tours, with Eleanor of Austria or the Duchesse d'Étampes, and loitering behind the hunting party rode the young Dauphin talking to the ever-juvenile Diana. The glimpses of gaiety which came ever and again to Chenonceaux during this reign, after the death of Francis grew in good earnest into that splendour and magnificence of which they were but the promise, and which never left it till the death of Catherine de Medicis. As the favourite of the King, the triumphant Diane de Poitiers was given outright that estate which she had

monarchie." The "two daughters of the horseleach" left these unlucky officials little rest.

no doubt coveted long before on the hunting excursions from Plessis-lez-Tours. The pretext of the gift consisted in the valuable services rendered to the State by her husband Louis de Brézé, Grand Seneschal of Normandy, services which it had remained for Henry II. to discover and reward. She was given all rights implied in the domain, and at Paris, at Tours, and at Amboise the deeds of gift were signed and countersigned.

But Diana did not yet feel safe. At the very outset of our acquaintance with her we shall find her fair fame tarnished with the intrigues and chicanery of a lawsuit, which had for its sole object the possession of a firm and inalienable right to the lands of Chenonceaux, to oppose to the inevitable objections of the envious Queen. Nor does this trait in her character appear fortuitously; to the very end Diana appears cold and hard. In the great famine of 1557 she gave no alms away to her starving tenants. Throughout her life she grasped at every chance of riches and preferment, and let very little slip.

This strange process now began. The inalienability of Crown property being still a question of some uncertainty, Diana determined to go back to the crisis of the unhappy Antoine Bohier's fate, the 28th of May 1535, to say that his calculations had been grossly exaggerated, and to completely annul the contract which had received the formal assent of the last King. But this was not all: the ill-used Bohier was then to be reinstated in a sarcastic mockery of ownership, and the balance of his old debt rigorously demanded; he would then inevitably be declared bankrupt, his lands put up for auction, all other bidders, even the Seigneur de Rochecorbon, conquered by the invincible favourite, and Diana should at last become the legal owner with incontestable rights. All this was done: the wretched General of Finances was crushed in every court of law, and though a Gentleman of the Royal Chamber, a Privy Councillor, and Lieutenant-General of Touraine, he was obliged to fly to Venice; the curse of his high office was upon him. Of the twelve men who had held this post since Marigny in 1315, eight had died violent deaths, three had been ruined, Florimond Robertet alone under Charles VIII. and Louis XII. had been unmolested and died quietly. Nor did the history of Bohier's own family contain much that was encouraging: Semblançay had been sacrificed, his wife's uncle, Jean Poucher, had been unjustly hanged, his cousin, Gilles Berthelot, had been exiled, and Azay-le-Rideau suffered the same fate as Chenonceaux.[1]

[1] The covetous and grasping Louise de Savoie was peculiarly hostile to the financiers. In the first years of her son's reign she writes: "Sans y pouvoir donner provision, mon fils et moi feusmes continuellement desrobés par les gens de finances;" and again, in 1518, "en Novembre le moine rouge, Anthoine Boys (Cardinal Bohier), parent de nostre reverendissime chancelier et des inextricables sacrificateurs de finances, alla de repos en travail hors de ce monde; et lors fut faict une fricassée d'abbayes, selon la folle ambition de plusieurs papes."

So Antoine Bohier fled, seeing no other alternative, but the parody of justice went on, adhering with a rigorous irony to all its forms. He let all its judgments go against him by default, until Diana had finally secured her Naboth's vineyard at (it is pleasing to notice) a considerably heightened price, until his famous balance had been for the second time forgiven, and he could return bearing with him the mockery of a forced approval and a heavy heart to begin life afresh.

While the new proprietress is arranging with De l'Orme[1] the plans of her new bridge across the Cher, is building her Italian gardens (to which every famous gardener in Touraine contributes), and planting her labyrinth within her park, we must take our stand, too, among the crowds of busy workmen by the river, and watch more closely the face that had so great an influence over Henry II. and the destinies of France.

It is a pale, untroubled face, with waving bands of raven hair above a brow of brilliant white, a face that will not easily grow old, for it has never suffered from emotion, that has outshone the painted countenances of all other beauties at the Court by the use of no other drugs than indifference and cold water.[2]

[1] It is certain that De l'Orme was at Chenonceaux in 1556 at any rate. He was disgraced three years afterwards, and in 1565 appeared his *Livre d'Architecture*, some time before Du Cerceau's more famous account of the *Plus Excellents Bastiments de France*.

[2] See Brantôme (ii. 395), who saw her in her old age, "aussy belle de face, aussy fraische, aussy aymable comme à l'aage de trente ans."

Diana, born in 1499, was the daughter of Saint Vallier, whose plots with the Constable had been punished by imprisonment at Loches. At fifteen she married Louis de Brézé, Seneschal of Normandy, the grandson of a traitor, and the son of a descendant of Agnes Sorel who murdered his adulterous wife.

For fifteen years the heat of the Rhone blood within her veins was tempered by her life in Normandy among the lawsuits and processes of her husband; her only appearance in the larger world was in connection with Saint Vallier's release, for the story of her amours with Francis I. was the invention of a scandalous Court and nothing more.[1] She remained unheard of till her husband's death, and then came quietly to Court with her two girls to marry, and the reputation of an impregnable widow. She consequently secured the highest prize of all; for Francis, half ashamed of the dull nature of his son, whose youthful spirits had been somewhat crushed and clouded in Spanish prisons, had laughingly recommended this sombre Dauphin to the good

[1] The details of her father's trial show this. See also Coignet, *Un Gentilhomme des Temps Passés*, cap. v., and Clement Marot's verses—

> "Que voulez vous, Diane bonne,
> Que vous donne?
> Vous n'eustes, comme j'entends,
> Jamais tant d'heur en printemps
> Qu'en automne."

Whether she knowingly aimed at the rising and left the setting sun is uncertain—she was quite clever enough to do so.

graces of the handsome Seneschale, who was to teach him courtly manners and a becoming affection for the Italian wife whom he had for so long neglected. And Madame Diane was keen enough to see the way to stir the sluggish spirit and undeveloped passions of the prince, who amid the gallantries of his father's idle Court had grown up uncared for and neglected.

"Though somewhat of a melancholic temper," says the ambassador Marino dei Cavalli, "he is yet very skilful in all arms and exercises; though slow of speech his thoughts are clear and his opinions sound; his mind has ripened slowly like the fruits of autumn." Thus it was that the Italian airs and graces of his young foreign wife had not appealed to him, but his slow heart opened out and gave itself irrevocably to the maturer charms of Diana in the pure black and white of modest widowhood.

Her strength, her magnificent health, the cold resolve and energy of her character, appealed to him as much as the firm line of her features, the proud curve of her lip, the narrow forehead which marked the decision of her nature rather than the loftiness of her ideas.[1] There was no sensuality, no tenderness

[1] See the portrait in the library at Aix, with the lines in Francis' handwriting, "Bele à la veoir, Oneste à la anter." There is another drawing in crayon in the Niel collection, a medal (in the Bibl. Nat.) with the legend, "Omnium victorem vici," and the statue at Versailles. These are without doubt authentic, and, as nearly as may be, contemporary. Many others of uncertain origin are at Rouen, at Chenonceaux,

in this face, nothing but the visible expression of strength of will and action, the serenity half divine that Goujon was to express in the exquisite lines of his "Diane Chasseresse" at Anet.

So calm and so impassive a divinity would already leave something to be desired by most men, but for a later age, that judges of her actions after the confusing magic of her countenance has passed away, there is a more serious defect. This woman who, by the very repression of her soul, kept firmer hold upon the stern régime that gave imperishable health and beauty to her body, was disfigured by a very demon of avarice and intrigue insatiable.[1] She took Anet, she took Chenonceaux, she took the Duchy of Valentinois, she laid hands on the very treasury of the new reign and kept the key. She had, it is true, inspired the delicate and artificial masterpieces of her time,[2] but her stately influence had chilled the impetuous spirit of the Renaissance; her nature is more reflected in the squares and spaces of the Italian garden than in the wild flourishes of the

at Chaumont, at Azay-le-Rideau, at Hampton Court. See M. Guiffrey, *Lettres inédites de D. de P.*

[1] "Grande véritablement," says Michelet, "énormément capace, miraculeusement absorbante. La baleine, le léviathan sont de faibles images."

[2] See the picture, belonging to the school of Clouet, from which in 1879 six copies were taken—of which there is one in Bibl. Nat. Gal. des Estampes. It is apparently of Diana in old age, still with the same *tight*, pale features. It adds a sinister association to the title of Valentinois, that the most famous holder of it in recent times had been the handsome and unscrupulous Italian, Cæsar Borgia.

turreted roof of Chenonceaux. Similarly, there is a cool calculation about her first entry into Court; the waves of scandal, even the outbursts of the astonished King, break unheeded against the stony rock of her indifference. She quietly and surely makes her way into the very depths of the Dauphin's affections, marries her daughters into the powerful families of Lamarck and Guise, and with yet more astounding subtlety of penetration wards off the possible opposition of Catherine de Medicis, by actually reconciling her disdainful husband to her presence, encouraging the backward Henry in his duties, and even watching over the sickbed of the mother and the cradles of her children. Her liaison with Henry[1] was not to be reproached with jealousy at any rate, for she had recognised only too keenly the necessities of her own position, and of the politics of the time: the only two friendships which the Dauphin had permitted himself before Diana had appeared were with Montmorency and with his brilliant playfellow, Saint André: both were very shortly firm friends of Diana.[2] In the last years of Francis,

[1] To the very end she persisted in representing it as nothing more than a Platonic friendship.

[2] In the Bibl. Nat. Man. fr. 3021, fo. 94, and 3139, fo. 63, are two letters from Diana to the Constable—in the first of which occurs the regular treaty of alliance between them. "Assurez vous Monsyeur," she writes, "que sy vous voulez ainsy user en mon endroit, comme me mandez, je vous seray sure et obeyssante comme personne au monde."

It is interesting to note how two such different characters were united by their common interests; yet the sombre faith of the Constable, with

distracted as we have seen by the strife of parties and intrigues, the party of Diana was the strongest, the party that was coming to the throne, and her influence over the new King became the more invincible that from her skill and tact it was almost unfelt.[1]

The reign of Henry II. began, as it ended, with a tournament. The transition between the times of Francis to the new society of the last Valois was signalised by a reversion to the older world which settled its differences in the trial by combat. This

his terrible "paternosters" interspersed with sudden orders for a hanging or a quartering forthwith, was not so very different in its results from the mocking cynicism with which Diana suppressed her own religious convictions, and refused to listen to her conscience. Dumas is probably right in hinting that there was an even closer tie between the pair than mere political alliance; yet it is hardly intelligible that the King could have had a serious rival in this brutal soldier who had as little good fortune when a general as he had good manners when a courtier.

[1] Unfortunately we have none of Diana's letters to the King, to explain in part the magic of her influence over him—several of his still exist. Bibl. Nat. Man. fr. 3143, fos. 2, 3, 4, 5. "Madame mamye, je vous remercye très humblement de la peyne que vous avez prise de me mander de vos nouvelles, quy est la chose du monde que je tiens la plus agréable, et vous supplye de me tenir promesse, car je ne puis vivre sans vous, et sy vous saviez le peu de passetams que j'ay vous auriez pityé de moy. Je ne fèré plus longue lectre, sinon pour vous asseurer que ne sçauriez sitost venir que le souhaite celuy qui demeure à jamés vostre très humble serviteur."

The letter is signed with the ⊟⊖ which so often recurs in the decorations of Chenonceaux; the cipher did as well for H and D as for the initials of Henry and his Queen Catherine. By the kindness of the Crédit Foncier, and of M. le Breton at Tours, I have been able to reproduce in this volume one of the rare examples of Diana's handwriting which exist, from one of the MSS. in the Archives of Chenonceaux; as was probable, it is a receipt.

strange scene of the duel between Jarnac and Châtaigneraie, sanctioned by the King himself, and watched by a multitude besides, has been often described ; for the details, which are interesting enough, we must refer the curious reader to the "procès verbal" of the duel.[1] The gist of the whole sad matter is put shortly in the pages of Vieilleville, and we have but time in this place to look quickly at the crowded lists for some indication of the spirit of the times we have to deal with. The quarrel had arisen on the misunderstanding of a word between the gallants of the Court that might have been at once explained away but for the bitterness of party spirit in the last years of the reign of Francis I. ; and now a " whole infinity of people from Paris, scholars, artisans, and vagabonds," had come to St. Germain en Laye to see the fight and discuss the chances of the champions. Châtaigneraie, thick-set and strong, with a large suite of followers behind him, the chosen gallants of that company of noble youths whom the King showed so proudly to the Venetian ambassador, with a gorgeous display of liveries and arms and banners, even a great tent spread with dainties for the anticipated victory, and crowded with plate borrowed from half the noble houses in Paris—Châtaigneraie seemed more than a match for the tall, thin, slightly-made Sieur de Jarnac, who had spent so long a time in the

[1] Bibl. Nat. Estampes, *Hist. de France*, reg. Q. b. 19. For Michelet's account see *Macmillan's Magazine*, No. 374, p. 130.

vulgar operations of making his will, committing his soul to God, and taking lessons from an Italian fencing-master.

To the sound of many trumpets the King appeared in the balcony above,[1] his face, naturally clouded, somewhat troubled with the thought of the risks his favourite was to run. Beside him are Diana and a brilliant suite of ladies in their Court costumes. But a long and wearying delay ensued, while the formal preliminaries were gone through. At last the combatants advance, and with one swift, sure stroke the famous "coup de Jarnac" has succeeded, and Châtaigneraie the boastful lies bleeding, with his leg half severed, on the ground. The King reluctantly approved the victory and moved sullenly back to the house of Baptiste Gondy nearer Paris. But all was not yet over. The crowd, angered already at their long wait, hungry, too, so far away from the good inns of Paris, and with half-understood feelings of resentment at the unfair attitude of the King and the haughtiness of the Court which had been thus unwittingly put on its trial, broke unrestrainedly through the fenced arena and sacked Châtaigneraie's tent. They pocketed the plate, they ate the delicacies raw, they trampled down the finery and furniture, and at last, not without sound scuffles with the archers of the guard, tramped back to Paris in the evening

[1] A miniature in the "Cérémonie des Gages de Bataille," a MS. in the Bibl. Nat., gives many details of a judicial combat such as this.

with no good opinion of the blessings of the opening reign. "Ainsi passe la gloire du monde qui trompe toujours son maître," moralises Vieilleville, "principalement quand on entreprend quelque chose contre le droit et l'équité."

The keynote of Henry II.'s character and of the years that were to come was struck with no uncertain sound. The France that had vigour enough to rise almost unharmed from the extravagances, the mistakes, the wars of Francis I., was crushed by the desperate folly of his son, by the gambling spirit of adventure which was the one alternative to the excesses of party struggle, by the fatal negligence and misgovernment which were responsible for the horrors of the Civil War and the unspeakable decay amidst which the last of the Valois was assassinated.

The reign of Henry II. never reached the dignity of a settled government. To the end it remained a bitter strife of parties, of Montmorencys against Guises or Châtillons. Guided by uncertain leaders, whose aims were for their own advancement, never for their country's, France looked for help where none was to be found, to Italy[1] and Scotland. In Scotland the Guises were already strong, and carried

[1] The siege of Sienna and the heroism of its defenders are described in the *Mémoires* of Montluc, who put off saying "ce méchant et vilain mot Je la rends" to the very last extremity. See also the account of the floods in Italy in 1558, and the antiquities laid bare by them, in François de Rabutin.

HENRY II., KING OF FRANCE, from the original picture by François Clouet in the possession of the Marquis de Biencourt at Azay-le-Rideau.

*Reproduced by permission of M. Péricat, Tours.*

out their policy by the marriage of their niece, Marie Stuart, to the Dauphin ; England was alternately flattered by Catholic alliances and disturbed by connivance with Protestant conspiracies, until in the reign of Elizabeth it was made definitely hostile by the tampering of the Guises with Scotland ; and for this Marie Stuart was to pay the penalty.

Within the kingdom the energies that should have been applied to State affairs were consumed in opposition to the power of Diana, and in the counter-moves of her supporters. Catherine attacked the situation with her characteristic methods. A fête was got up at St. Germain with Marie Stuart to adorn it, and a certain Miss Fleming whose fresh beauty served to attract the King for a season from the duchess ; but the youthful Scotchwoman was no match for the widow, and fresh measures soon became necessary. The Cardinal de Lorraine was at this time filling the rôle of Georges d'Amboise and Briçonnet, and a fresh conquest of Italy was attempted by way of diversion, but it failed as usual, and the Cardinal only succeeded in making an enemy of his ancient benefactress, Diana, who was strong in the support of Montmorency the Constable. Yet another mistress was produced to tempt the heart of royalty to fresh distractions, one Nicole de Versigny, who was to reproduce in later generations the intrigues and chicanery of Henry's Court, in the person of that Jeanne de Saint Remy who should give such unpleasant notoriety to a land-holder in Touraine, "the mud volcano" Cardinal de Rohan, the unwilling hero of the diamond necklace.

But more serious events occurred at last, and with them appeared the one pure figure in this shameful age, the Admiral Coligny, whose life is one long censure of the shams and debauchery of his contemporaries. At St. Quentin he was sacrificed by the mismanagement of Montmorency,[1] and the triumph of the Guises was still further assured by the taking of Calais from the English.

"It was time for the party of Reform to fight or die;" the party that fought for Shakespeare and for Bacon, for Rembrandt and Spinosa, for Descartes in France; the party which had already taken a firm hold on the intellectual sympathies of the nation, and which had already seen the blood of the first martyrs to its faith.[2] With the whole extent of this

[1] See the account of the siege in François de Rabutin, who also describes the taking of Calais.

[2] See the *Journal* of Louise de Savoie, 26th Sept. 1522. "Pierre Piefort . . . fut bruslé tout vif, après que, dans le donjon du chasteau il eut eu la main coupée, pour ce que impiteusement il avoit pris le corpus Domini, et la custode qui estoit en la chapelle." These early outbreaks of the Reformers excite less sympathy than their later sufferings. Francis I. was much troubled by their disorderly proceedings in Paris. But the movement to which they first gave organised expression had already attracted a certain amount of notice in high places (though not with any appreciation of their strength and meaning; see the chapter on the Conspiracy of Amboise). In December of the same year Louise writes: "Mon fils et moi par la grace du Saint Esprit commençasmes à cognoistre les hypocrites blancs, noirs, gris, enfumés, et de toutes couleurs, desquels Dieu par sa clémence et bonté infinie, nous veuille préserver et deffendre."

movement it is impossible to deal here, except in the cases where its results and its chief lessons are prominently brought before our eyes, as they are at Amboise and Blois. The horrors that were to come [1] were foreshadowed in the terrible scenes behind the Sorbonne in 1557, in the inquisitorial power given to the Cardinal de Lorraine ; and in the Edict of Ecouen. Diana, with the King at her side, had already seen the shrieking Protestants raised half-consumed out of the flames to be continually lowered into them again until the human cinder ceased to palpitate.

But of all this Chenonceaux knew nothing, and before leaving the troubles and the tortures of this mistaken reign we must turn, by way of contrast, to watch the life of the Court in this palace by the Cher, before Diana's light is put out and a new mistress comes to take her dwelling-place.

[1] For accounts of the movement by contemporary writers see Pierre de la Place, *État de la Religion et de la Republique*, also D'Aubigné's *Martyrologie*, and the writings of the Bourgeois de Paris, in MS. in the Bibl. Nat., fonds du Puy, No. 742, from 1515 to 1536, and published by M. Lalaune.

It is a simple and exact enumeration of facts without much comment, like the earlier Journal of the reigns of Charles VI. and Charles VII.

# INDEX

[NOTE.—The Appendix has been omitted in the references of this Index, and all but the more important of the notes.
A number, *e.g.* 34, refers to p. 34 of vol. i.; when vol. ii. is meant it is referred to thus: ii. 34.]

END OF VOL. I

*Printed by* R. & R. CLARK, *Edinburgh*